INTERNET PROTOCOL 6

INTERNET PROTOCOL 6

JULIE C. GAFFIN
EDITOR

Novinka Books
An imprint of Nova Science Publishers, Inc.
New York

For permission to use material from this book please contact us:
Telephone 631-231-7269; Fax 631-231-8175
Web Site: http://www.novapublishers.com

Library of Congress Cataloging-in-Publication Data:
Available Upon Request

ISBN 13 978-1-60021-349-6
ISBN 10 1-60021-349-9

Published by Nova Science Publishers, Inc. ✢ New York

CONTENTS

PREFACE*

The President's National Strategy to Secure Cyberspace (National Strategy) directed the Secretary of Commerce to form a task force to examine the most recent iteration of the Internet Protocol, IP version 6 (IPv6). The President charged the task force with considering a variety of IPv6-related issues, including the appropriate role of government, international interoperability, security in transition, and costs and benefits.

The Internet Protocol (IP) is an international communications standard that is essential to the operation of both the public Internet and many private networks in existence today. IP provides a standardized "envelope" that carries addressing, routing, and message-handling information, thereby enabling a message to be transmitted from its source to its final destination over the various interconnected networks that comprise the Internet.

The current generation of IP, version 4 (IPv4), has been in use for more than 20 years and has supported the Internet's rapid growth during that time. With the transformation of the Internet in the 1990s from a research network to a commercialized network, concerns were raised about the ability of IPv4 to accommodate anticipated increasing demand for Internet addresses. In 1993, the Internet Engineering Task Force (IETF) began a design and standardization process to develop a next generation Internet Protocol that would address, among other issues, the predicted exhaustion of available IPv4 addresses. The resulting set of standards, collectively known as IP version 6 (IPv6), was developed over the course of several years. Although various aspects of these protocols continue to evolve within the IETF, a stable core of IPv6 protocols emerged by 1998.

---

* Extracted from Technical And Economic Assessment Of Internet Protocol Version 6 (Ipv6), U.S.Department of Commerce.

This report by the Department of Commerce's IPv6 Task Force examines the technical and economic issues related to IPv6 adoption in the United States, including the appropriate role of government, international interoperability, security in transition, and costs and benefits of IPv6 deployment. In developing this report, the Task Force, with the assistance of a consultant, RTI International (RTI), has gathered information from a wide range of stakeholders through a request for comment published in January 2004, a public meeting held on IPv6 issues in July 2004, and numerous contacts with public and private-sector stakeholders.

The public record compiled by the Task Force suggests that although IPv6 has the potential to produce significant benefits for U.S. businesses and consumers over time, the near-term benefits are less clear. Available evidence suggests, for example, that in the initial years of IPv6 deployment, network security will likely be no greater under the new protocol than is currently available in IPv4 networks. Additional evidence suggests that premature adoption of IPv6 (i.e., that which precedes adequate technical and business case planning) could result in unnecessary costs and reduced information technology (IT) security.

The Evolving IPv6 Market and Potential Benefits

Although IPv6 is in the early stages of adoption, most network hardware, operating systems, and network-enabled software packages (e.g., databases, email, etc.) will likely include IPv6 capabilities within the next five years. In many cases, these IPv6 capabilities will be bundled as standard features of new versions of products, and thus will be incorporated in deployed networks through the usual cycle of replacing or upgrading hardware and software. This gradual deployment of IPv6 may occur at a somewhat faster pace in other countries, in large part due to perceived regional concerns about a shortage of IPv4 address space.

Industry stakeholders and Internet experts generally agree that IPv6-based networks would be technically superior to the common installed base of IPv4-based networks. The vastly increased IP address space available under IPv6 could potentially stimulate a plethora of new innovative communications services. Deployment of IPv6 would, at a minimum, "future proof" the Internet against potential address shortages resulting from the emergence of new services or applications that require large quantities of globally routable Internet addresses.

Current market trends suggest that demand for unique IP addresses could expand considerably in future years. The growing use of the Internet will likely increase pressures on existing IPv4 address resources, as more and more people around the globe seek IP addresses to enjoy the benefits of Internet access. In addition, the potential development of new classes of networked applications (e.g., widely available networked computing in the home, the office, and industrial devices for monitoring, control, and repair) could result in rapid increases in demand for global IP addresses.

Over time, IPv6 could become (as compared to IPv4) a more useful, more flexible mechanism for providing user communications on an end-to-end basis. The redesigned header structure in IPv6 and the enhanced capabilities of the new protocol could also simplify the configuration, and operation of certain networks and services. These enhancements could produce operations and management cost savings for network administrators. In addition, autoconfiguration and other features of IPv6 could make it easier to connect computers to the Internet and simplify network access for mobile Internet users.

Obstacles to IPV6 Deployment

Deployment of IPv6 faces a number of hurdles. First and foremost, the large embedded base of IPv4-compatible equipment and applications, coupled with the fact that IPv4 has proven to be robust enough and flexible enough to serve the needs of many producers and users, will likely constrain the rate of migration to IPv6. Additionally, in order to fully realize the potential end-to-end communications capabilities of IPv6, users will have to expend capital and labor resources to transition to the new protocol.

As a result, the transition to IPv6 may be a long process. Experts predict that long after most Internet users have migrated to IPv6, pockets of IPv4 may still exist in legacy systems. Hardware and software interoperability will be a key concern for enterprises wishing to interconnect their networks across heterogeneous environments. interoperability needs will be a major consideration in an enterprise's decision to adopt IPv6.

Economic Implications

Most observers generally agree that acquiring IPv6 capability over a short period of time will be more expensive than making the transition as part of a firm's normal upgrade/replacement cycle. IPv6 transition mechanisms and scenarios have been specifically designed to enable a prolonged overlap and to minimize deployment and operational interdependencies. Rather than forcing a short-term shift, many experts suggest that a reasonable deployment plan for Internet service providers (ISPs) and Internet users would focus on replacing as much IPv4-only hardware and software as possible through normal product refresh cycles. Activating IPv6 for routine use can effectively occur only after a critical mass of IPv6-enabled replacement technology, appropriate operational and security plans, and substantial training are in hand.

Most observers expect that ISPs and users will purchase IPv6-capable products during their normal equipment refresh cycles and that the costs of those products will be no greater than the costs of similar IPv4-only products. As a result, most of the costs that ISPs and users incur in turning on their IPv6 capabilities should be labor-related (e.g., staff training, installation, network testing).

Transition costs also will likely vary significantly among user groups. Costs to smaller Internet users, including residential users and small and medium enterprises (SMEs) that do not operate their own significant network services, will be relatively minimal if IPv6 capabilities are acquired through routine upgrades. In contrast, large and mid-sized user organizations, such as corporations and government agencies, will likely incur greater costs. The magnitude of those costs will depend on each user's existing network infrastructure and operational policies, the extent to which their custom applications must be modified to adopt IPv6, and whether the user intends to connect to other organizations using IPv6.

Security in Transition and in the Longer Term

The greatest potential security benefits of IPv6 appear to be associated with the long-term evolution of new security paradigms that are significantly different than those commonly employed in today's networks. In particular, evolving from today's network centric (perimeter- based) security architectures to end-to-end (host-based) models would better accommodate the self organizing systems envisioned for future network environments. The time and expense of designing and developing new security models will likely be considerable, but the creation of new, effective security paradigms would benefit all current and future Internet users.

With respect to IPv6 deployment in the near term, experts generally agree that implementing any new protocol, such as IPv6, will entail an initial period of increased security vulnerability. Additional resources will be necessary to deal with new threats posed by a dual standard environment. For example, while IPv6 may provide operational advantages over IPv4 with respect to auto-configuration and other capabilities, the new protocol's fundamental reliance on those capabilities also creates new threats and vulnerabilities associated with their potential misuse. Emerging new threats and vulnerabilities would clearly need to be addressed. Moreover, as IPv6 becomes more prevalent, many security issues will likely arise as attackers give it more attention.

Nevertheless, because IPv6 capabilities increasingly are included in new hardware and software products, IPv6 will likely begin to appear in operational networks independently of an organization's own plans and schedules for adoption. As a result, all organizations will need to develop security plans and policies for dealing with IPv6 traffic, regardless of their decisions whether and when to transition to IPv6. Although IPv6 transition mechanisms have been carefully designed for specific interoperability scenarios, operating in a dual standard mode will increase security risks. Users will likely need to devote additional resources to develop large-scale test and evaluation capabilities, to evaluate the impact of various transition mechanisms on typical security architectures, and to establish best common practices for new security policies and management mechanisms capable of ensuring the security and stability of networks in transition.

Thus, in the short term (i.e., in the first three to five years of significant IPv6 use), the user community will likely see no better security than what can be realized in IPv4-only networks today. Given its state of evolution, during this period, more security holes will probably be found in IPv6 and its transition mechanisms than in IPv4. In the longer term, security may improve as a result of increased use of end-to-end security mechanisms.

Potential Roles of Government

The Task Force finds that no substantial market barriers appear to exist that would prevent industry from investing in IPv6 products and services as its needs require or as consumers demand. The Task Force, therefore, believes that aggressive government action to accelerate deployment of IPv6 by the private sector is not warranted at this time. The Task Force believes that, in the near term, private sector organizations should undertake a careful analysis of their business cases for IPv6 adoption and plan for the inevitable emergence of IPv6 traffic on both internal and external networks.

With respect to public sector information systems, the Task Force recommends that government agencies initiate near-term activities to analyze their own business cases for IPv6 and to develop appropriate security plans for the inevitable emergence of IPv6 on both internal and external networks. This need for expedited planning and analysis in federal IT systems has also been identified in a recent report by the General Accountability Office and emerging policy guidance from the Office of Management and Budget. Each of these recommendations emphasizes that careful planning, development, and evaluation should precede any agency-specific decision to deploy new IPv6 technologies in operational networks. The results of this study indicate that significant technical and economic risks can be associated with failure to adequately plan for and appropriately schedule IPv6 adoption.

Looking longer term, the Task Force notes that the federal government will need to consider allocation of new resources and to work cooperatively with non-federal authorities and the private sector to address outstanding IPv6 research and development issues, and to expedite the development of suitable deployment, coexistence, and transition plans.

Chapter 1

INTRODUCTION

The President's National Strategy to Secure Cyberspace (National Strategy) directed the Secretary of Commerce to form a task force to examine the most recent iteration of the Internet Protocol version 6 (IPv6). The President charged the task force with considering a variety of IPv6-related issues, "including the appropriate role of government, international interoperability, security in transition, and costs and benefits."[1] Formed in October 2003, the Task Force is co-chaired by the Administrator of the National Telecommunications and Information Administration (NTIA) and the Director of the Technology Administration's National Institute of Standards and Technology (NIST) and consists of staff from those two agencies, with the assistance of a consultant, RTI International (RTI).

IPv6 merits study because of the growing importance of the Internet in the life of most Americans. Over the past decade, the Internet has revolutionized computer and communications activities. First envisioned as a tool for facilitating interaction among government and academic researchers, the Internet now touches almost every aspect of society. It has vastly expanded the individual and societal benefits of personal computers by becoming the primary mechanism for the dissemination, retrieval, and exchange of information between and among millions of computer users worldwide.

The social effects of these developments have been immense. The Internet has enabled consumers to shop more conveniently, choose from a wider selection of products and vendors, and customize their purchases. As a result, consumers spent $69.2 billion online in 2004, a 24 percent increase from 2003 and up more than 150 percent from 2000.[2] Similarly, the growth of online distance learning classes and medical reference Web sites has given people greater access to educational and medical resources. Government agencies and organizations can more easily process requests from and make information available to citizens, thereby facilitating interaction between citizens and government and reducing the costs to government of providing essential services.[3] The Internet also creates opportunities for individuals to participate more fully in the marketplace of ideas that is the foundation of American democracy.

The Internet's effects on the economy have been equally profound. Although the Internet has helped increase competitive pressures in many product and service markets, it has also equipped many businesses to thrive in the new market environment. Internet-based electronic mail and business-to-business software applications have enabled companies to reduce transaction costs, increase managerial efficiency, and improve the ways in which they transmit billing, inventory, and other information. That, in turn, has allowed companies to bring better products to the market more quickly and at lower cost. In these and other ways, the Internet offers businesses the opportunity to manage the entire technology life cycle more efficiently from product or service development to operations and maintenance.

The United States has played a major role in the development of the networks, standards, and conventions that make up the Internet, and Americans have become major users of IP-based services. As a result, the United States has been and continues to be a major beneficiary of the Internet revolution. Americans' extensive use of the Internet has contributed to the robust performance of our economy over the last decade, both in absolute terms and relative to other nations. America's central role in the creation and operation of the Internet has also put U.S. companies on the cutting edge of information technology (IT) markets, which have been a primary engine of economic growth and job creation domestically over the last decade. For these and many other reasons, the United States has a substantial interest in the future evolution of the Internet and in ensuring that U.S. firms can continue to participate fully in that evolution and its economic spillovers.

1.1. The Internet Protocol and IPv6

This report focuses on one of the communications protocols[1-4] that define the infrastructure of the Internet — the so-called Internet Protocol (IP), which enables data and other traffic to traverse the Internet and to arrive at the desired destination. IP not only provides a standardized "envelope" for the information that is sent; it also contains "headers" that provide addressing, routing, and message-handling information that enables a message to be directed to its final destination over the various media that compose the Internet.

The current generation of IP version 4 (IPv4), has been in use for more than 20 years and has supported the Internet's growth over the last decade. With the transformation of the Internet in the 1990s from a research network to a commercialized network, concerns were raised about the ability of IPv4 to accommodate emerging demand, especially the anticipated demand for Internet addresses. As a result, an international organization, the Internet Engineering Task Force (IETF), began work on the next generation IP. Its efforts led to the development of IPv6.[5]

IPv6 will enable an enormous increase in the number of Internet addresses currently available under IPv4. Demand for such addresses will increase as more and more of the world's population request Internet access. Cisco Systems notes that if the 15 largest countries were to assign unique addresses to only 20 percent of their populations, the resulting demand would easily exhaust the remaining supply of IPv4 addresses.[6] Continued growth in mobile data services via wireless telephones and data terminals, such as personal data assistants (PDAs), will also expand demand for Internet addresses. The situation may become critical if, as some project, a market emerges for in-home devices (e.g., "smart appliances" and entertainment systems) that are accessible from outside the home via the Internet.[7] Although considerable disagreement exists as to whether, to what extent, and at what pace, such demand will develop, it is expected that deployment of IPv6 would provide the address space to accommodate whatever level of demand does emerge.

Besides affording exponentially expanded address space, IPv6 has been designed to provide other features and capabilities, including improved support for header options and extensions, simplified assignment of addresses and configuration options for communications devices, and additional security features. Development of IPv6, moreover, has stimulated enhancements to IPv4. As useful capabilities have been devised for IPv6, protocol developers and manufacturers have worked to incorporate a number of those same capabilities into IPv4.[8] As a result, IPv4 can now support, to varying degrees, many of the capabilities available in IPv6.[9] At the same time, additional mechanisms and tools have been developed to mitigate, to an extent, the IPv4 address exhaustion concerns that in large part prompted the development of IPv6.[10]

Most observers agree that, all things being equal, IPv6-based networks would be superior to IPv4-based networks. As noted above, IPv6 would adequately accommodate increased demand for IP addresses in the event that a proliferation of end-user devices or the emergence of a "killer application" outstrips the existing supply of IPv4 addresses.

In the United States, however, there is a massive embedded base of IPv4 equipment and applications in the communications system we know as the Internet. The capabilities of IPv4, which have been enhanced over time in response to the development of IPv6, make IPv4 functionality sufficient to serve the needs of many current Internet users and service providers. Consequently, an important policy question concerning IPv6 deployment in the United States is whether the incremental benefits of adopting IPv6 justify the costs of converting the large embedded IPv4 base to IPv6 on an accelerated basis (e.g., well in advance of an organization's normal equipment replacement cycle).[11]

Because of conversion costs and the complexities involved in predicting a return on investment for IPv6 in the short term, most observers believe that there will be a considerable transition period during which IPv4 and IPv6-based networks will coexist.[12] During that transition, firms will incur costs to ensure interoperability among equipment, applications, and networks, both domestically and to a lesser extent internationally. Simultaneous operation of IPv4 and IPv6 may also require additional effort to ensure communications security and to protect networks from attack. These transition costs, in addition to the more obvious direct costs of converting to IPv6 and making any other necessary network changes, should be considered when assessing the benefits of adopting IPv6. Enterprises must determine whether the cumulative benefits of deploying IPv6 will justify the costs of migrating from IPv4 to IPv6.

1.2. Current Market Activities

1.2.1. Domestic Market Activities

Many domestic and foreign companies have incorporated or are steadily incorporating IPv6 capabilities into their hardware and software products. The two largest manufacturers of Internet routers, Cisco and Juniper, have included IPv6 capability in their equipment for several years.[13] Linux operating systems are generally capable of handling IPv6 traffic ("IPv6-capable"),[14] and Microsoft has moved aggressively to make its operating systems IPv6-capable.[15] Indeed, Cisco estimates that about one-third of desktop computers currently deployed in the United States are IPv6-capable.[16]

Microsoft is working to make more of its Windows applications capable of handling the larger IPv6 addresses,[17] and today consumers can download a limited selection of e-mail programs, multimedia software, remote access software, games, and Java applications that can operate in an IPv6 environment. Similarly, access software, email and World Wide Web servers, and firewalls are available that enable network administrators and users to interact with both IPv4 and IPv6 applications.[18]

Despite the availability of IPv6 products in the marketplace, a significant portion of the installed base of IT equipment in the United States, particularly in residences, appears to be capable of handling only IPv4 transmissions.[19] Furthermore, IPv6 has not been enabled, or activated, in much of the installed IPv6-capable equipment and software.[20] In June 2003, the United States Department of Defense (DoD) announced that all hardware and software "being developed, procured, or acquired" for its Global Information Grid (GIG) would have to be IPv6-capable beginning on October 1, 2003.[21] However, DoD apparently does not plan for the GIG to handle significant quantities of IPv6 traffic for several years.[22]

The bulk of the IPv6 traffic in the United States appears to be carried by government and university research networks, such as the Abilene backbone network.[23] Currently, NTT/Verio is the only commercial provider of IPv6-based Internet access service in the United States.[24] The company estimates that less than one percent of the Internet access users in the United States have IPv6 service.[25] MCI has announced that it has established a direct, high-capacity link between its commercial Internet backbone network and the Moonv6 test bed established by the North American IPv6 Task Force (NAv6TF), in collaboration with DoD and the University of New Hampshire.[26] This capability allows MCI's customers to test the performance of IPv6 equipment and applications as part of the Moonv6 test bed over native IPv6 links. MCI views this move as preparing its backbone network to deliver IPv6 capabilities on a more commercial scale. Currently, the company provides customized IPv6 services on a limited basis in North America, Europe, Africa, and the Middle East.[27]

1.2.2. International Market Activities

Commercial adoption of IPv6 is proceeding faster in other parts of the world, although market statistics are not readily available. NTT Communications began offering commercial IPv6-based Internet access service in Japan in March 2000. An NTT competitor, Internet Initiative Japan (IIJ), followed suit in September 2000.[28] NTT/Verio reports that Telecom Italia Laboratory was the first company to provide commercial IPv6 service in Europe in July 2001.[29] Juniper indicates that several other companies are conducting commercial pilots in other parts of Europe.[30]

Foreign governments, particularly those in Asia, have taken various steps to promote deployment of IPv6. Japan's support for IPv6 dates back to September 2000, when Prime Minister Yoshiro Mori emphasized the importance of IPv6 research.[31] In 2001, the South Korean Ministry of Information and Communication announced its intent to implement IPv6 within the country. In September 2003, the Ministry adopted an IPv6 Promotion Plan that commits $150 million through 2007 for funding IPv6 routers, digital home services, applications, and other activities.[32] In December 2003, the Chinese government issued licenses and allocated $170 million for the construction of the China Next Generation Internet (CGNI), with the goal of having that network fully operational by the end of 2005.[33]

For its part, the European Commission (EC) in 2001 funded a joint program between two major Internet projects—6NET and Euro6IX—to foster IPv6 deployment in Europe. The Commission committed to contribute up to €17 million over three years to enable the partners to conduct interoperability testing, interconnect both networks, and deploy advanced network services.[34] The EC has also allocated €180 million to support some 40 IPv6 research projects on the continent.[35] Finally, the EC is conducting a three-year, €10.7 million experiment with IPv6 networks that include household sensors for monitoring maintenance and meter reading. Sensors in automobiles could also be networked so that information about traffic and road conditions can be shared between vehicles.[36]

1.3. Department of Commerce IPv6 Task Force

Much of the IPv6 market activity internationally, particularly that in Asia, seems attributable to perceived shortages of IPv4 addresses.[37] However, some have said that foreign governments also see a swift transition to IPv6 as a way to gain a competitive advantage in the equipment and applications markets.[38] This, in turn, has raised concerns about the pace of IPv6 deployment within the United States and whether a "lag" in U.S. deployment could jeopardize the competitiveness of domestic firms in cutting-edge IT markets or have adverse security implications for this country.

To address these and other concerns about deployment of IPv6 in the United States, in January 2004, the Task Force published a Request for Comments (RFC) on various IPv6-related issues in the Federal Register.[39] In July 2004, based on the comments submitted in response to the RFC, as well as on extensive contacts with private- and public-sector stakeholders, the Task Force published a discussion draft that offered preliminary views on the questions presented by the ongoing deployment of IPv6 both domestically and internationally, including those issues identified in the National Strategy.[40]

On July 28, 2004, the Task Force convened a public meeting to examine IPv6 issues, including the discussion draft.[41] The information gathered at that meeting affirmed and supplemented many of the impressions set forth in the discussion draft and suggests that IPv6 has the potential to produce significant benefits for U.S. businesses and consumers. The vastly increased IP address space available via IPv6 could stimulate a plethora of new communications devices, all accessible directly by other Internet users on an end-to-end basis. That, in turn, could spur development and deployment of innovative services and applications. Over time, IPv6, as compared to IPv4, could become a more useful, more expandable mechanism for securing communications on an end-to-end basis.

Notwithstanding these potential benefits, deployment of IPv6 faces a number of hurdles. First and foremost, a large embedded base of IPv4-compatible equipment and applications exists, coupled with the fact that IPv4 has proven to be robust enough and flexible enough to serve the needs of many users and equipment/service suppliers. Additionally, full exploitation of the technical advantages of IPv6 will require not only capital and labor resources to transition to the new protocol, but also changes in the architecture of many user networks, including the removal or modification of devices that can interfere with end-to-end communications and the development of new security models. As a result, many firms may decide that the benefits of deploying IPv6 may not justify the costs, at least in the near term.

No substantial market barriers appear to exist that would prevent firms from investing in IPv6 products as their needs require or as consumers demand. As a result, the Task Force believes that aggressive government action to accelerate private sector deployment of IPv6 is unwarranted at this time. In terms of the public sector, the record indicates that IPv6 is increasingly being incorporated into Internet hardware and software. Consequently, the Task Force believes that federal agencies should initiate near term, focused, efforts to plan and operationally prepare for the increasing availability and use of IPv6 products and services in both internal and external networks. The vital importance of early planning efforts to ensure the safe and economic emergence of IPv6 within federal networks is also highlighted in emerging policy guidance from the Office of Management and Budget (OMB)[42] and a recent study by the Government Accountability Office (GAO).[43]

Pursuant to the President's directive, this report addresses a variety of issues related to a move to IPv6. Section 2 assesses the potential benefits of IPv6 adoption, as compared to IPv4, as well as the principal direct and indirect costs that entities will likely incur to deploy IPv6. Section 2 also provides an assessment of the sorts of costs that stakeholders may incur to deploy IPv6. Section 3 discusses the potential security benefits of IPv6, as well as the possible hurdles to the full achievement of those benefits. Section 4 considers issues related to the interoperability of IPv4 and IPv6 equipment and networks, including interoperability across national borders. Finally, Section 5 examines possible rationales for U.S. government action to influence domestic IPv6 deployment, and describes actions that the U.S. government should take to (1) facilitate adoption of IPv6 by government agencies and (2) assist the private sector in identifying and addressing potential barriers to smooth and efficient implementation of IPv6 by the private sector.

Chapter 2

BENEFITS AND COSTS OF ADOPTING IPV6

Industry stakeholders and Internet experts generally agree that IPv6-based networks[44] would be technically superior to IPv4-based networks. The increased address space available under IPv6 could stimulate development and deployment of new communications devices and new applications, and could enable network restructuring to occur more easily. The redesigned header structure in IPv6 and the enhanced capabilities of the new protocol could provide significant benefits to Internet users, network administrators, and applications developers. IPv6 could also simplify the activation, configuration, and operation of certain networks and services.

Widespread adoption of IPv6, however, could entail significant transition costs because the Internet today is composed almost entirely of IPv4-based hardware and software. Furthermore, as noted above, many of IPv6's enhanced capabilities have also been made available in IPv4, albeit with varying levels of performance. As a result, producers and consumers may continue to use IPv4 for some period of time (perhaps with further augmentation) to avoid or to defer the costs of upgrading to IPv6. Many of the prospective benefits of IPv6, moreover, appear to be predicated on the removal or modification of "middleboxes" that affect direct Internet communications between end-user devices, such as Network Address Translation (NAT) devices (see Section 2.1.1.2), firewalls, and intrusion detection systems (IDS). It remains to be seen whether or when such devices will be either phased out or made transparent to end-to-end (E2E) Internet communications and applications.

In this section, we discuss the benefits and costs of adopting IPv6. After first evaluating the potential benefits of deploying IPv6, we discuss the nature and relative magnitude of the costs that enterprises and individuals may incur to deploy IPv6. To make this general discussion more concrete, we also provide a case study in Appendix A that illustrates potential transition costs for a small or medium-sized business. Finally, we discuss transition issues and costs that are of particular importance in assessing the net economic impact of adopting IPv6.

2.1. Relative Benefits of IPv6 vs. IPv4

A general consensus appears to exist regarding the technical improvements of IPv6 versus IPv4 and the types of benefits that could follow from widespread adoption of IPv6. Disagreement exists, however, regarding the size of those benefits and whether the incremental benefits of IPv6 (versus IPv4) for some or all users would outweigh the costs of a greatly accelerated transition from IPv4 to IPv6.[45] This section discusses the potential net benefits of adopting IPv6, as identified by RFC commenters, RTI's discussions with industry experts, the available literature, and participants at the July 28, 2004 public meeting.

2.1.1. Increased Address Space

A principal by-product of deploying IPv6 would be a large increase in the number of available IP addresses. The 32-bit address field in the IPv4 packet header provides about 4 billion (4x109) unique Internet addresses.[46] The 128-bit address header in IPv6, in contrast, provides approximately 3.4x1038 addresses, enough to assign trillions of addresses to each person now on earth or even to every square inch of the earth's surface.[47]

The vast pool of addresses available under IPv6 would, at a minimum, "future proof" the Internet against potential address shortages resulting from the emergence of new and unforeseen services or applications that require large quantities of globally routable Internet addresses.[48] Pressures on existing IPv4 address resources will likely increase in coming years, as more and more people around the globe seek IP addresses to enjoy the benefits of Internet access.[49] The burgeoning demand for "always-on" broadband services (e.g., DSL and cable modem services) and the expected proliferation of wireless phones, wireless data devices (e.g., PDAs), and eventually wireless video services may further deplete the available IPv4 address space.[50]

Further, if consumers are drawn to devices that can be remotely accessed and controlled via the Internet and that require fixed, globally accessible Internet addresses (e.g., smart appliances, in-home cameras and entertainment systems, and automobile components or subsystems), demand for IP addresses may overwhelm the remaining pool of IPv4 addresses.[51] Although it is difficult to predict exactly when these developments may threaten the existing supply of IP addresses, the availability of virtually unlimited IPv6 addresses would enable Regional Internet Registries (RIRs) [52] and Internet service providers (ISPs) to accommodate any sharp spike in demand.

2.1.1.1. Improving Address Allocation

Adoption of IPv6 could provide an opportunity to reform and rationalize the current system for allocating Internet addresses, because deployment of IPv6 has created a vast new and unpopulated address space. The historical allocation of IPv4 addresses has provided organizations in North America, Europe, and Australia with the majority of currently assigned IPv4 address blocks. A large portion of those addresses remain unused. Although current allocation policies have improved, no incentives have been created to prevent "warehousing" of IP addresses[53] or to motivate the return of unused IP addresses. As a result, many organizations still have very large address blocks that have never been fully used and may never be reclaimed in the absence of concerted action by governments or by Internet registries.[54]

Deployment of IPv6 creates an opportunity to use the lessons learned from the past to adopt more efficient allocation policies for IPv6 addresses. On July 2, 2002, ARIN adopted IPv6 address allocation policies developed jointly with the Réseaux IP Européens Network Coordination Centre (RIPE-NCC) and the Asia Pacific Network Information Centre (APNIC). Policy 6.3.5 states that "[a]lthough IPv6 provides an extremely large pool of address space, address policies should avoid unnecessarily wasteful practices. Requests for address space should be supported by appropriate documentation and stockpiling of unused addresses should be avoided."[55]

Although concerns about IPv4 address exhaustion drove development of IPv6,[56] steps have been taken to conserve addresses and to improve the efficiency of address allocation.[57] As a result, a number of observers believe that the United States, Western Europe, and Australia may not experience address space concerns for some time.[58] Even in those areas of the world that are most concerned about potential exhaustion of IPv4 addresses (e.g., India and the Pacific Rim countries), some observers question whether the problem is so severe as to warrant accelerated adoption of IPv6.[59]

Additionally, in response to concerns about the perceived shortage of IPv4 addresses stemming from historical address allocation policies,[60] the RIRs have reorganized themselves in recent years to ensure that, prospectively, all regions are allocated IP addresses through a fair, transparent, and efficient process.[61] IPv4 address blocks are currently allocated to the RIRs from a common global pool, using agreed upon criteria and methodology.[62] When a region requests more addresses, they are allocated to the RIR on a need-justified basis.[63] As a result of these changes, the regional distribution of remaining IPv4 addresses now mirrors the global distribution of IP networks themselves. Consequently, the allocation scheme should no longer be the cause of any perceived regional shortages of IPv4 addresses.[64]

To capture fully the address benefits of IPv6, those entities involved in the process should continue working to ensure that IPv6 addresses are allocated fairly and efficiently.[65] The North American IPv6 Task Force (NAv6TF) indicates that some organizations have had trouble getting IPv6 addresses recently and suggests that allocation procedures may need to be changed so that IPv6 addresses can be obtained more easily. Otherwise, NAv6TF avers, widespread IPv6 adoption (and the potential associated benefits) might be stalled or precluded.[66] At the same time, VeriSign emphasizes the need for allocation policies that discourage "warehousing" of IPv6 addresses to prevent inefficient consumption of those addresses.[67]

2.1.1.2. Facilitating End-to-End Services and Applications

Proponents of IPv6 contend that the massive increase in IP addresses afforded by IPv6 deployment could stimulate development of innovative end-to-end (E2E) applications by eliminating the need for network address translation (NAT) equipment. A NAT is a device often placed between a private network and the Internet to allow a large number of hosts on the private network to share a smaller number of globally routable, "public" IP addresses for communications over the Internet.[68] For internal communication, each host is assigned a locally unique private IP address (see Figure 2-1).

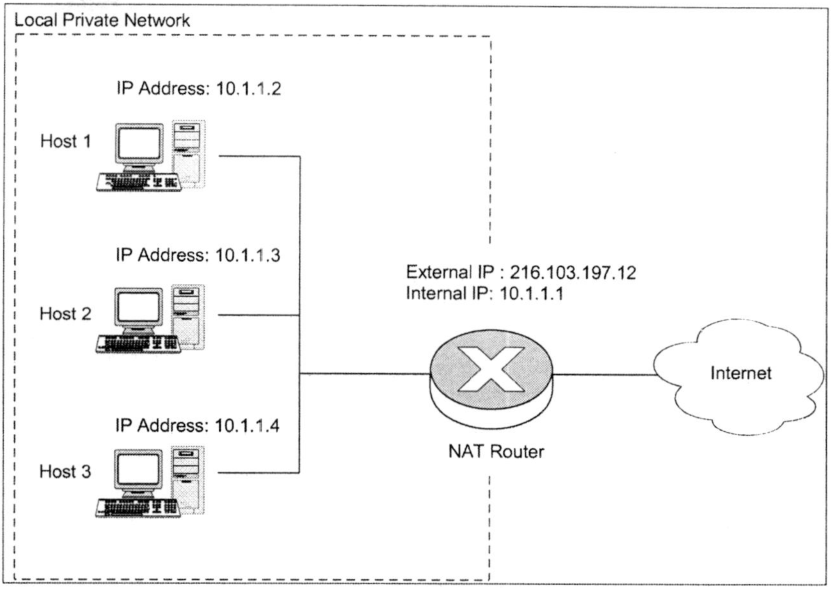

Source: RTI

Figure 2-1. NAT Operating between a Private Network and the Internet.

As the term implies, a NAT converts the private source address in outgoing communications to a globally routable IP address. In many implementations, an external address is assigned only for the duration of a communications session originated by an internal host, and the internal host cannot receive communications originated from the outside. Because NATs are an effective way for many hosts to share a single or a small group of public IPv4 addresses, they have proven to be a popular way to slow the consumption of IPv4 addresses. The massive increase in address space available under IPv6 would obviate the need for NATs as means of address conservation.[69]

Although, as discussed below, NATs provide some benefits for network administrators and end users, they also complicate the use and development of new E2E networking applications. One commenter suggests that the existing IPv4 infrastructure can be compared to the code of a large software application—after years of adding work-arounds and patches, it is sometimes simpler to replace the application and develop a streamlined program with which to move forward, rather than to continue patching.[70] Representatives of Nortel Networks have stated that designing the next generation of Internet applications will be simplified when using IPv6 because it avoids the more than 20 years of work-arounds embedded in IPv4, in part, to support E2E applications.[71]

To the extent that use of IPv6 obviates the need for NATs, adoption of IPv6 could stimulate the development and deployment of innovative E2E applications. This may occur because applications designers would be able to "focus on core products and services, rather than network logistics."[72] More specifically, designers could avoid the time and effort needed to develop work-arounds (also known as NAT transversals) that enable specific E2E applications to operate in a "NATed" environment.[73] These work-arounds may not scale well in all environments,[74] may reduce the performance and robustness of the associated applications, and may increase the cost and complexity of network management.[75] In their view, if designers are not distracted by the need for NAT work-arounds, new services and applications could be brought to market quicker and at a lower cost.

Without NATs, moreover, applications such as Voice-over IP (VoIP) and real-time videoconferencing could be implemented much more simply, because a direct connection (i.e., IP address to IP address) could be initiated to any host, without the need to establish additional protocols and procedures to traverse one or more NAT devices.[76] Some commenters assert that without NATs, various features of IPv6, such as connectivity via a wider range of media and delivery mechanisms, the ability to maintain several simultaneous access paths for multiple parties without manual intervention, improved speed, and quality of connections, could spur the deployment of new E2E applications.[77]

Indeed, advocates contend that widespread deployment of IPv6 and a concomitant removal of NATs would permit a return to the original "open scheme" of the Internet, based on E2E connectivity.[78] Devices that are globally addressable so that they can be remotely accessed and controlled on an end-to-end basis via the Internet represent a huge potential application of IPv6 addresses. Automobile components or subsystems, refrigerators, cameras, computers, and other home appliances could be assigned unique IP addresses, linked together on home networks, and connected to the Internet, so that home owners could control such devices remotely. In general, IPv6 offers opportunities for wireless sensor networks and for machine-to-machine communications, potentially leading to a large proliferation of devices that will connect to the Internet.[79]

The growth in such individually addressable and controllable devices and subsystems could, among other things, increase the life expectancy of large ticket items such as automobiles and appliances (durable goods) due to remote monitoring of these items' operation to determine preventive servicing requirements with the result of a decrease in service/repair costs. RTI estimates that if such remote monitoring could extend the life expectancy of an automobile or appliance by only one percent, and reduce service costs for those items by one percent, the potential economic benefits to society could exceed $3 billion per year.[80] To the extent that the benefits from this one type of E2E application are achievable by other types of applications, the overall economic gains could be substantial.

Despite the potential benefits of unlimited IP addresses and a NAT-less world, adoption of IPv6 may not prompt a return to the "open architecture" originally envisioned by the designers of the Internet. It has been noted, for example, that the E2E Internet model was developed in a very specific environment—one characterized by a relatively small number of sophisticated users working in trusted relationships towards a common purpose.[81] Today, the commercialized Internet operates in a very different environment—tens of millions of users, most of whom have no connection or affinity with other users. Some of those users, moreover (e.g., hackers, snoopers, and spammers), are working at cross-purposes with other users. Little evidence exists to suggest that, in this more wide-open Internet environment, a substantial number of network administrators would want to return to a network design that will enable any other Internet user to connect with them on an end-to-end basis.[82]

Although NATs were not designed to, and thus cannot provide, reliable security, their use in conjunction with local addressing schemes can conceal users to some degree from unwanted communications.[83] Because NATs generally preclude outside parties from initiating communications with host devices sitting behind a NAT, they can help block many of the common virus and worm probes that are constantly scanning the Internet for vulnerable hosts. By so doing, NATs can provide a limited form of "security through obscurity," thereby enabling network operators to block externally initiated contacts and to hide internal hosts.[84] It remains to be seen how similar effects will be achieved with IPv6 technologies. Ongoing design and specification work for IPv6 "Network Architecture Protection" and "Unique Local IPv6 Unicast Addresses" are attempting to address some of these issues.

More importantly, concerns about security in the Internet environment have prompted organizations to deploy a range of "middleboxes" (e.g., firewalls, intrusion detection and prevention systems) that, like NATs, may inadvertently affect or purposely inhibit E2E communications. Those devices have become essential elements of most current enterprise networks and are commonly used to enforce network security policies that have emerged since the Internet was first developed.[85] Few, if any, network operators will be likely to remove those devices should they decide to implement IPv6, at least in the absence of tools or techniques that can reliably provide an equivalent level of security in an E2E world.[86] Consequently, most observers believe that, even if NATs were to disappear tomorrow, many devices would remain in place that could impede the smooth development and deployment of E2E services and applications.[87]

In short, the ability to exploit the virtually unlimited IPv6 address space to support a growing number of networked devices or to stimulate the development of innovative E2E Internet applications and services will likely be limited by several relevant factors—a continuing supply of IPv4 addresses, possible difficulties with obtaining IPv6 addresses, a potential reluctance to eliminate NATs, firewalls, and middleboxes that affect E2E applications,[88] and an absence of compelling applications that require E2E connectivity.

2.1.2. Simplified Mobility[89]

Mobile services and mobile users could be major beneficiaries of the massive address space available via IPv6. Various commenters anticipate a rapid growth in the potential number of mobile or portable devices that may connect to the Internet. NTT/Verio notes that the use of mobile phones for email and database browsing in Japan has been growing rapidly. [90] Sprint suggests that the emergence of mobile data services such as wireless data, picture mail, and text messaging could drive the adoption of IPv6.[91] Motorola argues further that IPv6 offers exciting opportunities for wireless sensor networks and for machine-to-machine communications, potentially leading to a large proliferation of devices that will connect to the Internet.[92]

Quite apart from IPv6's address benefits for mobile services, many experts believe that, whether used in a mobile or a portable environment, IPv6 can better support such devices than currently available options under IPv4.[93] According to Microsoft, "IPv6 better handles mobile applications and services."[94] The North American IPv6 Task Force suggests that IPv6 allows devices to attach to networks at different points more easily than is currently achievable using IPv4 alternatives, principally through the use of stateless address autoconfiguration and neighbor discovery capabilities.[95] Sprint suggests that IPv6 will permit more optimal routing of mobile traffic because IPv6 mobility specifications are being designed to eliminate "triangular routing."[96]

The simplification of mobile networking in IPv6 could enable Internet users to remain seamlessly connected and easily reachable when portable or mobile devices move from their home networks to other unaffiliated networks.[97] The possibility of continuous Internet connectivity for laptops, mobile phones, PDAs, sensors, and other mobile or portable devices, in turn, could spur development of myriad new applications in both the public and private sectors.[98]

2.1.3. Improved Quality of Service (QoS)

Internet transmission currently is a "best effort" scheme—users cannot expect that "high priority" traffic will be handled any differently from other traffic.[99] For business IP-based services to flourish, service providers will likely need to provide Quality of Service (QoS)[100] support for those customers. This would require, among other things, the ability to identify different classes of traffic and to provide sufficient instructions to the connecting networks so that messages are delivered with acceptable performance characteristics (e.g., error rates, delay).

Several commenters suggest that, as presently implemented, IPv6 provides no better QoS support than does IPv4.[101] Nevertheless, the IPv6 packet header contains a field—the "flow label"—that is not found in IPv4 and that is intended to assist with QoS. The flow label allows a user or provider to identify those traffic flows for which the provider requests special handling by network routers with greater specificity (or "granularity") than is available under IPv4.[102] The expanded capabilities of IPv6 are not yet available to users and service providers, however. According to IETF RFC 2460, "There is no requirement that all, or even most, packets belong to flows, i.e., carry non-zero flow labels [such as QoS] . . . [and] protocol designers and implementers [should] not assume otherwise."[103] One expert has indicated, however, that "without the flow label and hop-by-hop option processing of IPv6, [optimal QoS operations] would not be possible."[104]

The IETF has begun to develop standards and specifications that would allow users and service providers to exploit the potential benefit of the IPv6 flow label. In March 2004, it released a foundation document that specified the flow label field and identified minimum requirements for IPv6 source nodes that wish to label packet flows, for IPv6 routers forwarding labeled packets, and flow state establishment methods.[105] Additional work will be needed to build on these basic requirements to create flow label specifications for particular uses, such as QoS.[106] It, therefore, appears that significantly more work is needed before a mature QoS standard is specified and, in turn, the potential QoS benefits of IPv6 can be realized.

Another constraint on the wide scale implementation of QoS, either in IPv6 or IPv4, would be the lack of QoS support in any one network segment of the transmission path.[107] Such a deficiency could negate QoS gains realized in the rest of the network path. Further, from a commercial standpoint, service providers will not offer QoS support unless the offered differential in service quality translates into increased revenues from customers (i.e., if QoS utilization translates to improved service for the user and higher revenue for the provider).

2.1.4. Reduced Network Administration Costs

Experts have suggested that IPv6 will reduce network administration costs in the long run if enterprises reorganize their networking structure and operating processes to take advantage of IPv6's capabilities and remove NATs from their networks.[108] For example, the autoconfiguration feature available in IPv6 can simplify the connection of hosts and other devices to the Internet, thus reducing management overhead for network administrators.[109] The vast number of addresses available under IPv6 could simplify (and thus reduce the costs of) subnet management because each subnet could be given substantially more address space than the number of nodes that could be connected to it.[110]

If adoption of IPv6 motivates an organization to dispense with NATs, network administrators could more effectively use ping, traceroute, and other tools to diagnose network problems or to debug applications between pairs of hosts.[111] Removal of NATs could also simplify use of multivendor networking solutions.[112] Furthermore, decreasing the number of processing functions in a network (e.g., by eliminating NATs) could reduce the number of components that can fail, increase network resilience, and reduce management complexity and support costs.[113]

To the extent that the administrative cost savings of IPv6 depend on the removal of NATs, however, the potential savings may be constrained or even negated by the likely persistence of those devices in an IPv6 environment. More generally, immediate reductions in administrative costs flowing from adoption of IPv6 will likely not exist,[114] although the cumulative savings should eventually exceed transition costs. Many networks may not see a net reduction in costs for at least five or more years after initial IPv6 deployment, depending on the priority assigned to upgrading of systems, specific network complexities, and other issues that may arise during transition.[115]

Additionally, some experts have stated that aggregate administrative reductions will not be realized because new IPv6 issues related to new/advanced applications and projected increases in Internet traffic could incur added costs, including additional administrative activities.[116] However, this development still implies a decrease in the cost per unit of information exchanged.

In summary, during the extended transition period in which both IPv4 and IPv6 support will be required, total operational expenses (OPEX) for network operations will likely increase, rather than decrease. Any OPEX cost reduction will probably not be realized until significant operational experience has been gained at all levels of the network, including the application developer and user levels. This may not accrue for ten or more years.

2.1.5. Increased Overall Network Efficiency

Removing NATs, firewalls, and middleboxes, and/or restructuring network routing mechanisms (and administrative activities) would likely result in fewer processing steps and reduced transmission bottlenecks.[117] The change to a fixed header size in IPv6 could yield processing efficiencies, and deployment of IPv6 could also allow routing tables to be reduced in size and redesigned for maximum efficiency.[118] Some experts have said that such benefits will result only when IPv6 use is widespread.[119] The potential increase in overall network efficiency, moreover, may be difficult to correlate with adoption of IPv6. A much better benchmark, and the metric of greatest interest to the user community, is whether the performance of E2E and other applications improves significantly when using IPv6 transport.

Table 2-1. Overview of IPv6 Benefits

Benefits	Magnitude of Potential Benefits	Timing Issues	Likelihood of Occurrence	Key Factors in Realizing Benefits of IPv6
Increased address space	Large	No near-term shortage in U.S.	Medium/High	Removal of NATs; growth in number of end-to-end and other applications
Simplified mobility	Large	New applications will likely flow from Asian test markets	Medium/High	Growth/demand for new applications
Reduced network administration costs	Modest	Cost may increase during transition	Medium (in the long term)	Removal of NATs
Improved overall network efficiency	Modest	Efficiency may not improve until after large scale transition	Low	Removal of NATs
Improved QoS capacbilities	Modest/Small	Few benefits in the near future	Low	Ongoing standardization and subsequent implementation of QoS "flow label" field

Source: RTI estimates based on RFC responses and discussions with industry stakeholders.

2.1.6. Summary

As the foregoing discussion indicates (and as Table 2-1 summarizes), adoption of IPv6 can potentially produce measurable benefits for users, equipment vendors, and service providers. The largest likely benefits will be realized in the areas of increased address space (and associated innovations in services and applications) and improved mobility. Additional work must be done (e.g., removal of NATs, restructuring of networks, and standards setting) to fully capture the potential benefits. Although the long-term benefits may be considerable, the short-term benefits for many organizations may not exceed the costs of moving from IPv4 to IPv6 on a greatly accelerated basis.

2.2. Stakeholder Costs of Adopting IPv6

The potential costs associated with deploying IPv6 consist of a mixture of hardware, software, labor, and miscellaneous costs.[120] The transition to IPv6 is not analogous to turning on a light switch; instead, many different paths to some level of IPv6 deployment can be forged. Each organization or user throughout the Internet supply chain will incur some costs to transition to IPv6, primarily in the form of labor and capital expenditures required to integrate IPv6 capabilities into existing networks.

Expenditures and support activities will vary greatly across and within stakeholder groups depending on their existing infrastructure and IPv6-related needs. By and large, ISPs offering service to large groups of customers will likely incur the largest transition costs per organization, while independent users will bear little, if any, costs.[121] Factors influencing these costs include:

- the type of Internet use or type of service being offered by each organization;
- the transition mechanism(s) that the organization intends to implement (e.g., tunneling, dual-stack, translation, or a combination);
- the organization-specific infrastructure comprised of servers, routers, firewalls, billing systems, and standard and customized network-enabled software applications;
- the level of security required during the transition; and
- the timing of the transition.

Table 2-2 provides a list of relative costs that may be incurred by stakeholder group and gives a percentage breakdown by cost category. Table 2-3 provides an item-by-item list of the costs to deploy IPv6 by stakeholder group. This is a relative comparison of costs and should not be interpreted as representing the actual size of each stakeholder group's cost. Further, small Internet users (e.g., home and small businesses) are not captured in Table 2-3 because they will likely incur virtually no costs. Small Internet users will receive software upgrades (e.g., operating systems and email software) as new versions are purchased, that their IPv4-only hardware (e.g., routers and modems) will be replaced over time as part of normal upgrade expenditures, and that IPv6 will eventually be provided at no additional cost.[122]

Table 2-2. Overview of Relative IPv6 Costs

Stake-holders		***Transition Cost Breakdown***[a]			***Timing Issues***	***Key Factors in Bearing Costs***
	Relative Cost	Hardware (HW)	Software (SW)	Labor		
Hardware Vendors	Low[b]	10%	10%	80%	Currently most are providing IPv6 capabilities	Rolling in IPv6 as standard RandD expense; international nterest and future profits incentivize investments
Software Vendors	Low/ Medium[c]	10%	10%	80%	Currently some are providing IPv6 capabilities	Interoperability issues could increase costs
Internet Users (large)	Medium	10%	10%	70%	Very few currently using IPv6; HW and SW will become capable as routine upgrade; enabling cost should decrease over time	Users will wait for significantly lower enablement costs or (more probably) a killer application requiring IPv6 for end-to-end functionality before enabling
Internet Users (small)	Low	30%	40%	30%	Availability and adoption schedules	With little money to spare, these users must see a clear return on investment (ROI)
Internet Service Providers (ISPs)	High[d]	15%	15%	70%	Very few offering IPv6 service; no demand currently; very high cost currently to upgrade major capabilities	ISPs see low or nonexistent ROI, high costs, and high risk

Source: RTI estimates based on RFC responses, discussions with industry stakeholders, and an extensive literature review.

[a] These costs are estimates based on conversations with numerous stakeholders and industry experts. Several assumptions underlie them. First, it is assumed that IPv6 is not enabled (or "turned on") or included in products and no IPv6 service is offered until it makes business sense for each stakeholder group. Hardware and software costs are one-time costs. Labor costs could continue for as long as the transition period and possibly longer.

[b] For hardware vendors producing high-volume parts that require changes to application-specific integrated circuits (ASIC), the costs could be very high and would not be offered until the market is willing to pay.

[c] Software developers of operating systems have and will incur a relatively low cost; however, application developers will incur greater relative costs, designated as medium.

[d] The relative cost for ISPs is particularly high if the ISP manages equipment at user sites, because premises equipment is more costly to manage and maintain.

Table 2-3. Relative Costs of IPv6 Deployment by Stakeholder Group [a]

Item	Hardware, Software, Service Providers	ISPs	Enterprise Users
Hardware			
Replace interfacing cards	H		M
Replace routing/forwarding engine(s) [b]	M	M	
Replace chassis (if line cards will not fit)		M	M
Replace firewall		M	M
Software			
Upgrade network monitoring/management software		H	H
Upgrade operating system		M	H
Upgrade applications c			
• Servers (Web, DNS, file transfer protocol FTP), mail, music, video. etc.)			L
• Enterprise resource planning software (e.g., PeopleSoft, Oracle, SAP, etc.)			H
• Other organization-specific, networkenabled applications			H
Labor			
R and D	M	L	
Train networking/IT employees	H	H	H
Design IPv6 transition strategy and a network vision	M	H	M/H
Implement transition:			
• Install and configure any new hardware	L	H	H
• Configure transition technique (e.g., tunneling, dual-stack, NAT-port address translation	M	M	M
• Upgrade software (see Software sectionabove)		L/M	L/M
• Extensive test before "going live" with IPv6 services		H	H
Maintain new system		M/H	M/H
Other			
IPv6 address blocks			L
Lost employee productivity [d]			
Security intrusions [e]		H	H
Foreign activities		M	M
Interoperability issues		M/H	M/H

Source: RTI estimates based on RFC responses, discussions with industry stakeholders, and a literature review.

[a] The relative designation (L = low, M = medium, and H = high) indicates the estimated level of cost to members of each stakeholder group. These costs are not incremental, but reflect differences in costs between stakeholder groups. The blank spaces indicate that a particular cost category does not affect all stakeholder groups.

[b] The "brains" of the router are commonly found on line cards.

[c] Portions of the first column, principally relating to software upgrades by hardware, software, service providers, is blank because the costs of these activities are reflected in the corresponding categories in the "Enterprise Users" column.

[d] Because of unexpected down-time during transition period.

[e] Based on unfamiliar threats.

As part of the discussion in this section we provide some insight into which stakeholder groups will end up bearing the costs and which are most likely to appropriate the benefits associated with IPv6.

2.2.1. Hardware, Software, and Service Vendors

Vendors that provide products and services include: networking hardware companies, such as router and firewall manufacturers; networking software companies, including operating system and database management application developers; and service vendors, including companies that offer training, service and support. Obviously, these companies will need to integrate IPv6 capabilities into their products and services, if they have not already done so, in order for IPv6 capabilities to be available to end users and ISPs. Once IPv6-capable products are installed in user networks and their labor forces have been trained, ISPs will be enabled to offer IPv6 service (see Section 2.2.2 infra for more on ISP costs), and users will be able to purchase IPv6-enabled devices and applications. Many companies in this category are already developing, and some are even selling, IPv6-capable products and services largely because of demand outside the United States (e.g., Asia).

Comments received suggest that the majority of the costs being incurred by hardware and software developers include labor-intensive research and development (RandD) costs and training costs.[123] These costs, however, have not been large enough to deter most of those companies from beginning to develop IPv6 products and capabilities. RandD activity has generally been conducted in small intra-company groups dedicated to developing IPv6-capable products with, to date, limited, small-scale interoperability testing with other hardware and software makers. Based on industry experience with the early deployments of IPv4 equipment, large-scale deployment may bring to light additional interoperability issues.[124]

The future cost of interoperability testing could be substantial, but such testing is essential if IPv6 is to become seamlessly pervasive. Without interoperability testing, IPv6 capabilities could have little practical use.[125] NAv6TF, in collaboration with the DoD and the University of New Hampshire, has launched the Moonv6 test bed, which has stimulated interoperability testing by U.S. and foreign vendors wishing to offer IPv6 products or services.[126]

In the next several years, foreign activities will likely affect IPv6 transition costs borne by hardware, software, and service vendors. Several commenters noted that, as foreign companies and corporations encounter and solve various deployment issues, U.S. vendors will see lower implementation costs.[127] As products mature, fewer vulnerabilities are found, thus lowering implementation costs. The United States is likely to benefit from the current experience being gained by foreign activities. A point of diminishing returns will likely be reached at some future date, however.[128] In addition, several commenters stated that substantial foreign competition could drive up the relative prices of U.S. companies' products and services because with less market share they would not be able to spread RandD and other costs across a large customer base.[129]

2.2.2. ISPs

ISPs comprise two main categories: (1) companies (e.g., AOL, Earthlink, and myriad smaller companies) that provide Internet access service to corporate, governmental, nonprofit, and independent Internet users and (2) companies that own and maintain the backbone hardware and software of the Internet (e.g., MCI, Sprint, ATandT). The categories overlap because companies that own the backbone Internet infrastructure (i.e., Category 2 companies) often provide Internet access service to customers, either directly or through a subsidiary. Today, most backbone transport networks have already upgraded their major routers and routing software to accommodate IPv6. As a result, providing IPv6 connectivity to customers who do not require additional equipment, service, or support would be relatively low cost. Consequently, this analysis focuses on those ISPs in Category 1 that have large customer service provision capabilities.

These ISPs will likely incur relatively high transition costs as they enable IPv6-capable hardware and software and work through system interoperability problems. To date, however, little demand has appeared in the United States for IPv6 services or applications.[130] As a result, given the costs to reconfigure networks, experts and industry stakeholders agree that U.S. ISPs are currently not positioned to realize a positive return on investment from large-scale offerings of IPv6 service.[131]

For Category 1 ISPs to offer a limited amount of IPv6 service, they would need to integrate some transition mechanism(s), such as tunneling.[132] The costs of doing so will probably not be large.[133] If several routers and service provisioning software are upgraded and limited testing is performed, IPv6 service could be provided to a limited number of Internet users today at minimal additional cost.

Currently, some of those ISPs are performing some limited testing.[134] Before ISPs elect to offer widespread IPv6 service, however, they will need assurances that current service offerings would not be affected in any way. Such assurances would likely require much more testing and significant additional hardware, software, and training costs,[135] possibly increasing the costs by 200 to 300 percent more than would be incurred for a more limited service roll-out, depending on the number of affected customers and the nature of an ISP's infrastructure.[136]

If IPv6-capable products and services being offered in foreign markets (e.g., Asia) are transferable to the U.S. market, those ISPs offering IPv6 services abroad will have absorbed some of the initial costs of developing deployment strategies for those products and services. A majority of RandD costs attributable to IPv6 implementation, like any other advanced technology, may be borne by early adopters. Thus, one possible scenario is that U.S. ISPs may be able to take advantage of the lessons learned overseas to roll out those products domestically at a lower cost than would have been the case if the U.S. ISPs had deployed those offerings first. Such costs, however, are not likely to be a dominant factor for most application services in the long run.[137]

In the United States today, NTT/Verio is currently the only ISP providing end-to-end IPv6 service.[138] NTT/Verio began their move to IPv6 as early as 1997, replacing and upgrading hardware and software components to be IPv6 capable. By spreading out transition costs, including hardware and software costs, training, and the development of network administration software tools, NTT/Verio has been able to upgrade for very little additional costs above standard upgrade, training, and testing costs.[139] Although the transition may not be as inexpensive for other ISPs, NTT/Verio's experience illustrates how careful planning can help reduce transition costs whether or not "first-mover" advantages are realized.

Most experts agree that a shift to IPv6 over a short period of time will be more expensive than making the transition as part of a normal life-cycle update.[140] Transition technologies were specifically designed to enable a prolonged overlap and to minimize deployment and operational interdependencies. Rather than forcing a short-term shift, many experts suggest that a reasonable deployment plan for ISPs and Internet users would focus on replacing as much IPv4-only hardware and software as possible through normal life-cycle updates. Over any period of acquisition, turning on IPv6 for routine use should only occur after a critical mass of IPv6-enabled replacement technology and training are in hand.[141]

Thus, until customers begin demanding IPv6 service, most U.S. Category 1 ISPs have little incentive to incur any major additional costs to transition; as such, in the short term, most ISPs are likely to continue testing IPv6 and offer limited IPv6 connectivity as requested. However, as more hardware and software become IPv6 capable through cyclical replacements, continued standardization efforts by the IETF,[142] and testing by many parties, these ISPs will probably be in a position to recoup investment costs associated with IPv6 service.

2.2.3. Internet Users

Costs to upgrade to IPv6 for Internet users vary greatly. Independent Internet users, including residential users and small and medium enterprises (SMEs) that do not operate servers or any major database software, will need to upgrade only networking software (e.g., operating systems), one or more small routers, and any existing firewalls to gain IPv6 capabilities. This cost will be relatively minimal if the hardware and software are acquired through routine upgrades.

Larger organizations, such as corporations, government agencies, and nonprofits, will incur considerably more costs than home or small network users. The relative level of these costs, however, will depend on existing network infrastructure and administrative policies across organizations, the extent to which a specific organization wants to operate IPv6 applications, and whether it intends to connect to other organizations using IPv6. This section will focus on these larger costs.

The magnitude of the transition costs is still uncertain because only a few test beds and universities have made large-scale transitions. According to officials at Internet2, the time and effort needed to transition their backbone to IPv6 was minimal, and no significant system problems have been encountered. However, Internet2 indicated that their experimental system was implemented and maintained by leading industry experts. It is unclear what issues might arise from implementation by less experienced staff.[143] Another commenter points out, however, that if normal upgrade cycles are assumed to provide IPv6 capabilities, transition costs will be limited to training and some reconfiguration.[144]

Internet users, as a whole, constitute the largest stakeholder group. The robustness of and diversity within this group demands a more detailed explanation of costs broken out by hardware, software, labor, and other costs.

Hardware Costs

Depending on individual networks and the level of IPv6 use, some hardware units can become IPv6 capable via software upgrades. However, to realize the full benefits of IPv6, most IPv4-based network hardware will need to be upgraded with IPv6 capabilities.[145] Specifically, high-end routers, switches, memory, and firewalls all will need to be upgraded to provide the memory and processing needed to enable large scale IPv6 use within a network at an acceptable level of performance. It is generally agreed that to reduce hardware costs, all or the majority of hardware should be upgraded to have IPv6 capabilities as part of the normal upgrade cycle (generally occurring every three to five years for most routers and servers, but potentially longer for other hardware such as mainframes).[146] At that time, IPv6 capabilities should be available and included in standard hardware versions. In the short term, replacement of some forwarding devices and software could be used to set up small-scale IPv6 networks.

Software Costs

Significant software upgrades will be necessary for IPv6 use; however, similar to hardware costs, many of these costs will be negligible if IPv6 capabilities are part of the routine requirements in periodic software upgrades147. Software upgrades include server software, server and desktop operating systems, business-to-business (B2B) software, networked database software, network administration tools, and any other organization-specific network-enabled applications. Currently, the main software costs that user organizations envision pertain to element management, network management, and operations support systems that are often network specific and will need revised software coding to adjust for IPv6. Given the anticipated growth in IPv6-capable software, it is likely that if Internet users upgrade their commercial application software in three or four years, they will acquire IPv6 capabilities. However, they will still need to upgrade their company-specific software.

Labor Costs

According to experts, training costs are likely to be one of the most significant upgrade costs,[148] although most view it as a one-time cost that could be spread out over several years. The magnitude of these training costs will, of course, depend on existing staff's familiarity and facility with IPv6. On a daily basis, the change in operating procedure for IPv6 will be minimal. Most network staff, however, will need some understanding of the required network infrastructure changes and how they might affect security or interoperability.[149] NAv6TF notes that the relative programming skills of software engineers at a particular company could substantially affect upgrade costs.[150] A company with more skillful programmers might have to hire one additional employee, while another might need three or four, during a transition period that could last five or more years. Additionally, increased network maintenance costs following IPv6 implementation could be more pronounced depending on the relative level of IT staff skills and technical understanding. Similarly, training costs should be minimal for large organizations with existing IPv6 expertise (e.g., universities).

For mid-size organizations where IT staff perform multiple functions, staff training could be a significant share of the IPv6 transition costs. If non-IT staff need to alter their activities based on IPv6 use, training will be necessary for them, though generally this should not occur.[151] If customers will be affected in any way, sales staff and any other employees who interact with customers periodically will need to understand the potential problems and benefits that could affect their relationships with customers.

Additional labor resources (e.g., personnel and/or time) will be needed to run testing activities, to install and configure new hardware, software, and transition mechanism(s), and to maintain the new dual-stack (i.e., IPv4 and IPv6) network. As the transition takes place, a more complex network will likely require additional network administration costs. For example, in a dual-stack network, two standards will have to be supported; thus, security intrusions will likely increase in the short term (attributable to a lack of awareness of or a lack of experience with IPv6 security "holes"). These costs would be highest in an expedited deployment scenario. Costs would be lower in a gradual migration scenario where much of the testing and problem resolution can be completed internally over an extended period or through shared initiatives.[152] For U.S. users and vendors, costs would also be lower in a scenario where the early deployment issues are encountered and resolved in foreign countries.[153]

2.3. International Competitiveness

The pace of IPv6 deployment in the United States potentially raises issues broader than the costs incurred by individual producers and users. For example, actions by governments in Asia and Europe to promote deployment of IPv6 in their countries suggest that those governments believe that their domestic firms may gain competitive advantages from early adoption of the new protocol. More specifically, some foreign governments appear to see an opportunity to use the development and deployment of IPv6 to strengthen their position in global IT markets, particularly in Internet equipment, software, and services.[154] Some U.S. stakeholders worry that if the United States loses its current technical and market leadership in the Internet sector, recapturing that position will be difficult.[155]

2.3.1. First-Mover Advantages

Companies that first introduce or adopt a particular technology ("first movers") may in some circumstances have the ability to create barriers to subsequent entry or to influence the adoption decisions of other companies.[156] By so doing, the first mover may be able to dominate the markets associated with that technology and generate monopoly profits.[157]

Some experts question whether first movers will be able to capture sustainable competitive advantages in Internet markets, including those for IPv6 equipment, services, and applications. In applications markets, for example, the rapid pace of technological advances makes sustaining first-mover technology or information advantages difficult.[158] In addition, the short life expectancy of Internet technologies and the regular replacement of hardware and software applications reduce lock-in costs, as long as legacy systems are not a major obstacle.

Moreover, deployment costs are typically higher for innovators and early adopters of new technologies compared to the costs for imitators and later adopters. In any RandD-intensive industry, information spillovers counter first-mover advantages.[159] If U.S. companies are able to learn from the international community's early IPv6 adoption activities, U.S. deployment costs may be lowered and lead to competitive products and services with lower entry costs. Finally, empirical research has shown that the greater learning curve requirements for first movers lead to higher failure rates for these first-to-market participants.[160]

On the other hand, while imitators can take advantage of "lessons learned" by the innovator, later entrants into the relevant markets still must acquire infratechnologies[161] and other infrastructure, appropriate skills, and market experience in order to be competitive in emerging markets. The cost advantage gained from "borrowing" an innovator's learning curve may or may not be sufficient to overcome the scale and installed base advantages that accrue to first movers. Moreover, successful imitation frequently requires time compression with respect to acquiring infrastructure and applications capabilities. As the economic analysis summarized in section 2.3 indicates, more rapid transition will likely raise costs and may do so to a greater extent than the amount of time compression.

2.3.2. First-Mover Advantage and U.S. Competitiveness

Judging from the published literature, the RFC comments, and the discussion at the July 28, 2004 public meeting, U.S. stakeholders are aware of first-mover concerns, but some question whether significant adverse potential competitive effects would ensue if the United States lagged behind other nations in deployment of IPv6.[162] At this time, most markets for IPv6 products and services are in their infancy. Until applications and services markets begin to mature, determining whether efficiency gains or learning curve effects will generate sustainable first-mover advantages will be difficult.

An important point for this analysis is the fact that first-mover strategies are usually discussed with respect to the benefits and costs of innovation in applications. However, the issue here is the evolution of a critical infrastructure—a standard. Standards provide several functions that enable innovation: 1) reducing variety (e.g., one standard versus several incompatible protocols), which thereby presents larger potential markets and thus economies of scale; 2) providing information (e.g., format and timing of message transmissions), thereby reducing the costs of innovation; 3) assuring quality (e.g., accuracy and assurance of message delivery); and 4) assuring compatibility/interoperability (e.g., seamless integration of subnetworks and applications), thereby realizing network externalities.[163]

Several parties voiced strong concern that other countries are advancing IPv6 at a much faster rate than the United States, and that without government action to stimulate or assist U.S. deployment, the United States could lose its leadership role in Internet infrastructure and applications markets.[164] Another commenter indicated that a lack of U.S. technical experience in new IPv6-based equipment and applications development could put domestic firms at a disadvantage, as other countries would be able to work without NATs and other IPv4 work-arounds.[165] Other commenters focused on resource constraints. If the transition to IPv6 in the United States lags behind the international community, U.S. vendors will need to allocate resources to support both IPv4 and IPv6 to a greater degree.[166] As a result, U.S. firms would have fewer resources to devote to IPv6-only products and services.

In addition, the lack of a robust standards infrastructure for IPv6 in the United States that would be available to potential first movers could conceivably act as a barrier to innovation because the inefficiencies resulting from continued use of the existing standard could significantly reduce expected profits. Conversely, the cost of implementing a new standards infrastructure (as discussed in Section 2.2 above) is substantial and not returnable to individual private firms. This situation raises a potential "chicken-or-egg" problem, although the IETF has attempted to eliminate such a concern by creating mechanisms to promote interoperability between IPv4 and IPv6 networks, thereby facilitating a gradual but reasonably efficient transition strategy.[167]

To help ensure against the possibility of substantial catch-up expenditures, several commenters suggested that government incentives could be used (e.g., tax breaks or grants) to help offset transition costs.[168] However, other stakeholders have warned that government incentives would be unwise because they might skew the natural path of technology development or interfere with ongoing activities in the commercial marketplace. These stakeholders prefer that government simply participate in the market by adopting IPv6 when it is beneficial to its own needs.[169]

This report finds that corporate or industrial users have yet to realize significant productivity benefits from operating IPv6 versus IPv4, and may incur higher costs from early adoption of IPv6.[170] When more advanced IPv6 applications become available that represent efficiency gains, U.S. companies should be sufficiently well-positioned via ongoing hardware and software upgrades to take advantage of these opportunities. As discussed in Section 5.1, no market failures have been identified that would limit rapid deployment of IPv6 once future applications emerge.

Chapter 3

SECURITY IMPLICATIONS OF IPV6

3.1. COMPARING IPV6 AND IPV4

A number of commenters contend that IPv6 will provide a greater level of security than is available under IPv4. NTT/Verio states that because IPv6 was "designed with security in mind," it is inherently more secure than IPv4, which does not have integrated security fields. [171] Other commenters note that support for Internet Protocol Security (IPsec) is "mandatory" in IPv6, but only "optional" in IPv4, which should lead to more extensive use of IPsec in IPv6 networks and applications. [172] BellSouth suggests that incorporating IPsec into the IPv6 protocol stack may reduce incompatibility between different vendors' implementations of IPsec. [173]

The virtually limitless address space available via IPv6 can also further network security. Many common IPv4-based network attack scenarios begin with "brute force" address and port scans of entire subnets, sites, or even the Internet as a whole. In typical IPv4 deployments, once an assigned address prefix is known, an attacker only has to scan between 28 subnet and 216 site addresses (about 250 and 65,500 addresses, respectively) to find every host device on that network. The 64-bit space for individual interface IDs in the IPv6 address structure, on the other hand, is so vast that brute-force scans of the available address space are practically impossible. [174]

To the extent that deployment of IPv6 can enhance network security, the potential benefits to organizations and individuals can be significant. However, empirical estimates of the cost of cybersecurity breaches vary widely because of differences in what is included in the cost estimates and disincentives for companies to publicly disclose the number of breaches or level of damage. Studies that focus on IT costs, such as the 2004 Computer

Security Institute/FBI Computer Crime and Security Survey, have reported total losses from cybersecurity breaches of approximately $142 million in 2004. [175]

The evidence gathered in the Task Force's examination of IPv6 indicates that several potential security benefits can be realized from the eventual adoption and use of IPv6 by government, the private sector, and the Internet as a whole. At the same time, the greatest potential security benefits appear to be associated with the long-term evolution to new security paradigms, significantly different than those commonly employed in today's networks. As a result, the potential security benefits outlined above must be balanced against what might be considerable costs to complete the design and development of new security models and the potential increased risks to incrementally deploy and transition to them in existing operational networks.

A number of factors may also limit the possible security benefits of IPv6 deployment in the near term. For example, although the expanded IPv6 address space may eliminate address and port scanning-based network attacks, network administrators may also lose the ability to perform brute-force address scans for the purposes of security auditing and testing. Many popular IPv4 security analysis tools are fundamentally based upon address scanning. Thus finding and identifying misconfigured or compromised hosts that are deliberately "hiding" on an IPv6 subnet may be as difficult as attacking them from the outside. This implies that in IPv6 networks both network administrators and would-be attackers must look elsewhere (e.g., DNS, server logs, neighbor discovery caches) to gather lists of active hosts.

Furthermore, although IPsec support is mandatory in IPv6, IPsec use is not. In fact, many current IPv6 implementations do not include IPsec. [176] On the other hand, though optional, IPsec is being widely deployed in IPv4. [177] There appear to be no appreciable technical differences in the way that IPsec is implemented in either protocol, and several commenters state that there are no significant functional differences in the performance of IPsec in IPv6 and IPv4 networks. [178] Any differences in performance are attributable to the presence of NATs in most IPv4 networks, which interfere with E2E communications using IPsec. [179] Thus, to the extent that NATs persist in IPv6 networks, they may reduce the security benefits available via the new protocol. [180]

Furthermore, experts generally agree that implementing any new protocol, such as IPv6, will be followed by an initial period of increased security vulnerability and that additional network staff will be necessary to address new threats posed by a dual network environment. [181] For instance, IPv6 provides support for various configuration capabilities (e.g., neighbor discovery, address auto-configuration, router discovery, renumbering) and control (e.g., path MTU discovery). [182] These capabilities are richer and better integrated than the auto-configuration capabilities typically found in today's IPv4 networks and, as noted above, should result in reduced administrative costs associated with the operation of large-scale networks and potentially more streamlined implementations of some protocol functions.

Although there are clear operational advantages to these autoconfiguration and control capabilities, IPv6's fundamental reliance on their operation also creates new threats and vulnerabilities associated with their potential misuse. This fact, coupled with a desire to support end-to-end (or host-based) security architectures in which trust among local network nodes is not assumed, requires that new levels of scrutiny be given to the security of the IPv6 Internet Control Message Protocol (ICMPv6) and its uses in neighbor discovery, and address auto-configuration. In addition, most IPv6 auto-configuration mechanisms make significant use of multicast, anycast, and scoped addressing capabilities. Care must be taken to ensure that network security systems limit the extent to which these new modes of addressing are not exploited as new attack vectors by compromised hosts. [183]

Additionally, IPv6 inherently supports modes of addressing other than unicast (e.g., multicast, anycast, scoped unicast) that are not typically found in IPv4 operational deployments. Although these new addressing capabilities present significant opportunities for the development of new network services, security mechanisms and practices for these new modes of addressing are not as mature or well understood as those for global unicast. Additional efforts are needed to develop security solutions for IPv6 that can enable secure multicast and unicast communications while at the same time ensuring that these capabilities do not create new vulnerabilities in the networks in which they are deployed.

Although IPv4 may have presented similar security concerns when first implemented, it currently benefits in its comparison with IPv6 from 20 years of identifying and addressing security issues. As IPv6 becomes more prevalent, many security issues will likely arise as attackers give it more attention. On the other hand, the experience gained from running IPv4 networks may help bring security levels in IPv6 networks up to the level of current IPv4 networks at a faster pace. [184]

3.2. REEVALUATING EXISTING SECURITY MODELS

More broadly, in order to fully use the capabilities of IPv6 and IPsec to provide security on an end-to-end basis, enterprises will likely need to reexamine their existing security models. [185] Most enterprises currently implement security measures at the perimeter of their corporate networks (e.g., with firewalls). Such deployments commonly consist of a very limited number of interconnection points where network links are typically partitioned into external (i.e., those that permit communications with the outside world), internal private, and internal public segments (e.g., for servers that are visible to and reachable from outside the protected network). Middle-box security devices sit at the intersection of each of these segment types carefully enforcing site-wide security policies, providing security services, and monitoring traffic for security events. [186] Virtual private networks (VPNs) (i.e., IPsec tunnels) are often used to securely connect one trusted network to another and NAT devices often are inserted to allow the internal-private parts of the enclave to use private addressing.

The advantages of perimeter-based security models are that they focus site security definition, management, enforcement, and auditing at a very limited number of points in the network. Typically, these perimeter security points are under the total control of enterprise security organizations and are some of the most highly maintained and monitored assets in enterprise network infrastructures. Centralized monitoring and audit functions also allow for easy integration with other corporate information assets such as equipment inventories, employee directories, and the like.

If an enterprise allows its employees to establish communications with non-enterprise users on an end-to-end basis, the enterprise will have to explore other approaches for securing its employees and the enterprise network from security threats. In fact, the growing importance and acceptance of mobile devices (e.g., laptops, PDAs, IP phones, sensors), self-organizing networks and systems (e.g., mobile ad hoc networks; service-oriented software architectures; and peer-to-peer systems), and environments with untrusted local links (e.g., public wireless access points, multi-access residential broadband) may compel organizations to explore end-to-end or host-based alternatives to their traditional perimeter security models. [187]

In either event, the enterprise will need to plan carefully to ensure that the new security model does not expose the enterprise to external threats. End-to-end security models are inherently more complex than perimeter-based architectures and, as security experts frequently point out, "complexity is the enemy of security." [188] To date, moreover, development and standardization of the security management infrastructures and enforcement technologies necessary to support host-based security architectures appear to be immature. In order to support hybrid, distributed models of security policy management, enforcement, monitoring and audit, considerable research and development remains to be done. As a result, design, standardization, and testing of commercially viable technologies for security policy information models, distributed enforcement mechanisms, distributed monitoring mechanisms, and auditing technologies probably must precede practical deployment of host-based security architectures in large scale environments.

A key to widespread use of IPsec is the creation of a public key infrastructure (PKI), which is necessary to effectively manage widespread IPsec operations. PKI is an important element in the combination of software, cryptographic technologies, and network services that enable individuals and enterprises to protect the security of communications sent over the public Internet. These mechanisms allow Internet users to validate the identity of each party to a communication or transaction, to verify that documents or communications have not been altered or corrupted during transmission, and to protect information from interception during transmission. [189]

Commenters noted that the current absence of PKI and associated trust models is a significant impediment to widespread use of IPsec. [190] In this regard, the social and business aspects of establishing identities and trust relationships (e.g., privacy concerns and legal considerations) may be more difficult to resolve than the technical issues. [191] Until these issues are resolved and the required security infrastructure is created (a process that could take several years), IPv6 is not likely to stimulate any more use of IPsec than IPv4 does today. [192]

The implications of IPv6 and IPsec deployment for law enforcement are similarly unresolved. The potential widespread use of IPsec to encrypt communications may reduce law enforcement agencies' ability to monitor criminal activities over the Internet, particularly when IPsec is used in conjunction with IPv6 mobility. [193] In term of network traceback capabilities, to the extent that deployment of IPv6 enables the assignment of static, globally unique IP addresses to more end-user devices, adoption of IPv6 could in theory enhance the traceability of illegal or harmful communications back to their source. [194] Nevertheless, IPv6 users could still employ numerous standard and non-standard techniques (e.g., auto-configured addresses, unique local address, NATs) to give themselves a similar degree of anonymity, and thus limit traceability of their communications. [195] As a result, deployment of IPv6 may not provide clear advantages over IPv4 regarding law enforcement's tracking of IP addresses.

Furthermore, IPv6 has a "privacy extension" option in its autoconfiguration feature that enables users to randomize their IPv6 addresses or to generate temporary addresses that are independent of the identification label embedded in user devices. [196] Such addresses are traceable to the ISP or customer demarcation point but are more difficult to trace beyond those points. As a result, it may be challenging for law enforcement authorities to trace a specific node or device as it moves between attachment points or over extended periods of time. [197] Authorities will have to develop new tools and procedures to address these potential problems. [198] Overarching these concerns, moreover, are the difficulties determining the origination point of a message that has "hopped" across multiple nodes of the globally-dispersed Internet.

3.3. Security in Transition

Security concerns about either IPv4 or IPv6 are not limited to the capabilities and vulnerabilities inherent in the individual protocols. As noted above, most experts believe that a number of years will be required before IPv6 becomes the dominant Internet protocol. As a result, enterprises assessing the merits of adopting IPv6 must also consider the security issues that will arise during the transition period when both IPv6 and IPv4 are being used.

Although IPv6 supports several mechanisms to facilitate interoperation among IPv4 and IPv6 networks (e.g., dual-stack, tunneling, and translation), each of those transition mechanisms was designed with specific scenarios and requirements in mind. Careful selection and control of their use in actual deployments is required to minimize security breaches. Enterprises that operate dual-stack equipment, for example, will have to address the vulnerabilities of both protocols. Dual-stack nodes may provide global IPv6 connectivity to systems that assume private IPv4 address semantics. Dual-stack operation can raise other security problems if consistent security policies are not created for both IPv6 and IPv4 traffic. If a firewall is not configured to apply the same level of screening to IPv6 packets as for IPv4 packets, the firewall may let IPv6 pass through to dual-stack hosts within the enterprise network, potentially exposing them to attack. [199]

Enterprises that achieve interoperability via tunneling could also expose themselves to external attacks and threats. IPv6 packets encapsulated in IPv4 tunnels could pass through IPv6 firewalls and launch attacks on IPv6 network host equipment. [200] Additionally, tunneling mechanisms that communicating parties do not have an active hand in establishing are susceptible to packet forgery and denial of service attacks. [201]

More work is required to incorporate IPv6-suitable requirements into existing IPv4 security architectures. Because IPv6 is a different protocol that raises different security issues than does IPv4, IPv6 security policies that are simply cut-and-paste translations of existing IPv4 policies will not be adequate. Careful evaluation and tests of security systems (e.g., firewalls, intrusion detection systems (IDS), auditing tools) should also be conducted to determine their capabilities to support both IPv4 and IPv6, as well as specific transition mechanisms. In particular, evaluation of firewall and IDS capabilities for deep packet inspection of tunneled and translated packet formats may be required. Such evaluations should include an analysis of the impact and support of multicast, anycast, and privacy addresses. Security test and audit tools that employ address and port scanning may need to be modified to deal with IPv6 address space issues.

Finally, organizations must develop security plans for dealing with IPv6 traffic, regardless of their decisions and schedules with respect to whether and when to transition to IPv6. IPv6 capabilities already exist in most networks with recent host and router deployments. The fact that IPv6 capabilities are shipped by default in many common host and router operating systems implies that they may be "turned on" at any time, either on purpose, by accident, or for malicious purposes. Some systems may ship IPv6, and/or any one of its transition mechanisms, enabled by default. On some existing platforms, enabling the IPv6 protocol automatically enables various transition mechanisms.

These realities, coupled with the fact that bad actors are rapidly adopting IPv6 and are already using it to initiate attacks and hide malicious processes and communications, suggest that all organizations should develop explicit plans to provide, or prevent, IPv6 communications. Failing to do so will create the real potential that IPv6 will appear and be used on an organization's networks either by accident or for malicious intent. [202]

Although none of these transitional security concerns are insuperable, organizations planning to implement IPv6 must be aware of them and develop the necessary security policies to address them. Although IPv6 transition mechanisms have been carefully designed for specific interoperability scenarios, there is still much to be learned about the practical impact of their deployments in large organizations. Additional resources will likely need to be devoted to the development of large-scale test and evaluation capabilities, to the evaluation of the impact of various transition mechanisms on typical security architectures, and to the development and documentation of best practices for new security policies and management mechanisms capable of ensuring the security and stability of networks in transition.

In summary, it is likely that in the short term (i.e., in the first three to five years of significant IPv6 use), the user community will at best see no better security than what can be realized in IPv4-only networks today. During this period, more security holes will probably be found in IPv6 than in IPv4, and IPv4 networks will continue to have at least the same level of security issues as they do currently. In the long term (i.e., 15 to 20 years after first significant IPv6 use), security may improve as a result of increased use of end-to-end security mechanisms. Such a result assumes that significant RandD investment and widespread changes in networking occur, particularly in network security architectures and security management mechanisms.

Chapter 4

INTEROPERABILITY

The transition to IPv6 will likely be a long process and may never attain complete penetration before the protocol becomes obsolete. Some experts predict that in 20 years most Internet users will be using IPv6, but that pockets of IPv4 will still exist as parts of legacy systems. [203] Some firms may not find it cost-effective to convert large segments of their existing systems. Hardware and software interoperability is, therefore, a key requirement for interconnecting networks across heterogeneous environments and thus will be a major consideration in an enterprise's decision to adopt IPv6.

The developers of IPv6 recognize the prospect of a lengthy transition period from IPv4 to the new protocol and have attempted to accommodate that fact. [204] They have created several mechanisms (e.g., dual-stack, tunneling, and translation) to enable networks using either or both versions of IP to communicate with each other. Those mechanisms are intended to eliminate deployment dependencies between and among vendors and networks and thereby to allow enterprises to decide when to adopt IPv6, if at all, based upon their own needs and goals, without regard to the decisions of other enterprises. [205] Interoperability will likely not be completely seamless in practice. Firms will have to address a number of issues in order to minimize interoperability problems during the transition from IPv4 to IPv6.

4.1. Interoperability Between IPv6 Hardware and Software Applications

Because IPv6 is an industry standard, hardware and software applications produced by different vendors in accordance with that standard should be interoperable. Put another way, there is nothing inherent in the protocol that should create an interoperability barrier. In general, experts believe that with international cooperation most implementation differences can be avoided, and in the long run, interoperability problems will be minimal because producers will quickly adjust to avoid any productivity losses from interoperability problems. To date, experience shows that no obvious problems arise in implementing the IETF standards for IPv6 because major operating system and router vendors already have implemented and periodically demonstrated interoperability. [206]

However, some experts believe that, in the short run, differences in the implementation of IPv6 could potentially lead to interoperability problems in some areas. [207] For example, the protocol allows proprietary functions to be incorporated in optional headers that could lead to incompatibility. Conformance questions, therefore, will need to be addressed. Experts believe that additional test beds and activities (such as testing activities currently being conducted as part of the Moonv6 test bed) are needed. In the absence of such action, future IPv6 products developed in one company might not be able to interact with those developed in another under the same general standards. [208] For these reasons, organizations should emphasize interoperability in any transition plan to minimize costs and efficiency losses.

4.2. Interoperability Between IPv4 and IPv6 Hardware and Software Applications

Interaction or intercommunication between IPv6-only and IPv4-only hardware and software applications creates potential interoperability problems. Before a host on one network can communicate with a host on another network, the originating host will first have to determine which protocol(s) the receiving host supports and then make the necessary arrangements to send a recognizable message. While to some extent these issues can be addressed through proper configuration and use of DNS entries and responses (e.g., identifying which hosts support IPv6, IPv4, and dual stacks), complexities in determining viable combinations of application, network protocol and transition mechanisms to use for a specific instance of communication still remain. While careful, robust application designs can resolve many of these issues, this process could increase delays or decrease network efficiency. Both networks could mitigate these interoperability problems by deploying dual-stack capability. The IETF has reported, however, that dual-stack equipment does not eliminate interoperability concerns. If an IPv6 node is placed in a mixed IPv6/IPv4 environment, it may encounter problems that lead to connection delays, poor connectivity, and network insecurity. [209]

Tunneling can facilitate interoperability between IPv6 and IPv4 networks, but it also increases packet overhead. Although that would not create undue hardship for network routers, it would increase processing time and network overhead costs. [210] The interoperability benefits likely outweigh the additional costs, however. Most importantly, interoperability mechanisms, such as tunneling, allow an enterprise to transition to IPv6 at its own pace, lowering hardware and software costs, and minimizing the impact on existing operations. [211] Nevertheless, a company must keep the costs of interoperability in mind, as it decides when and how to deploy IPv6.

4.3. International Interoperability

Interoperability issues also have an international dimension, including different levels of conformance and implementation strategies across countries and regions and the legal and privacy implications of encryption restrictions across countries. International interoperability issues associated with dual IPv4 and IPv6 network capabilities should be minimal because IPv4 is well-established globally and can be used as a network foundation; interoperability between IPv6 applications needs to be tested more extensively in an international context, however. Of particular significance to an international discussion is the impact of interoperability, or a lack thereof, on U.S. competitiveness both in Internet hardware and software and in other industries.

4.3.1. Interoperability Implications for U.S. Competitiveness in Internet Hardware and Software Markets

International interoperability problems generated by local standardization tactics of individual countries can create market barriers for U.S. hardware and software suppliers by raising the cost for U.S. companies to compete in international markets. As a result, at least one commenter suggested that U.S. government agencies must be prepared to defend the interests of U.S. firms by ensuring that IPv6 or IPv6-related standards established or implemented by other nations are open, transparent, and not anticompetitive. [212]

Even in a world where the international community cooperates to minimize interoperability problems, parallel ongoing development activities in Asia, Europe, and America will inevitably lead to interoperability issues, and companies that are active early in the process will have the opportunity to influence solutions and gain valuable experience. For example, to compete effectively in global markets for Internet router equipment, U.S. suppliers will need to provide leading-edge support for IPv6 both domestically and internationally. The development of the needed IPv6 capabilities may be constrained, however, if U.S. networks and services remain predominately IPv4-based.

One commenter suggested that to compete in a global market with interoperability issues, IPv6 deployment should be encouraged domestically so that American vendors can move up the learning curve more quickly and be competitive in international markets where IPv6 will be even more heavily (or more obviously) emphasized. [213] In other words, adoption of standards as a means of reducing interoperability problems, coupled with potential learning economies, are possible rationales for a more rapid transition to IPv6 in the United States.

4.3.2. Implications for U.S. Competitiveness of Market Timing Decisions

For U.S. vendors, the costs of developing and deploying products and services could be lower in a scenario where the early deployment issues are encountered and resolved in foreign countries. [214] Furthermore, continued reliance on an embedded base of IPv4 equipment should not preclude the United States from realizing the benefits of foreign IPv6 deployment, as long as a means exists to connect embedded IPv4 networks and applications to newly deployed IPv6 networks and applications. The developers of IPv6 have attempted to accomplish that goal by making IPv6 backwardly compatible with IPv4 via interoperability mechanisms.

However, some commenters indicated that an embedded base of IPv4 equipment and applications could function as a barrier that would isolate the United States from the benefits of foreign IPv6 deployments and/or test beds. [215] Forward-thinking entrepreneurs might not be able to develop new services based on IPv6 or may simply participate in the new markets emerging in other areas.

With respect to domestic innovation incentives, small and medium U.S. businesses have limited resources. Thus, if they encounter high costs due to partial IPv6 deployment domestically, or if foreign competition benefiting from learning economies elsewhere in the world penetrates the U.S. market, barriers to domestic innovation efforts could be significant. Incomplete deployment also may send inaccurate market signals and result in premature introduction of IPv6 products, which could be damaging to small and medium firms. [216]

Finally, in the transition to IPv6, one of the most important interoperability objectives is to ensure the security and stability of IP networks around the world. Therefore, any transition to IPv6 should move forward in a cautious and technology-sensitive way to minimize adverse effects for users. International standards development and coordination bodies should be used to vet technical issues pertaining to IPv6 migration and the coordination of interoperability issues.

Chapter 5

GOVERNMENT'S ROLE IN THE EVOLUTION OF IPV6

As discussed in Section 2, many of the original concerns motivating the development of IPv6, such as perceived address space limitations and security needs, may not be driving forces for rapid deployment of IPv6 in the United States, at least in the near term. That does not imply, however, that potential benefits of adopting IPv6 do not exist. Nor does it mean that a potential role for government does not exist with respect to influencing the realization of those benefits. The public comments, discussions with industry stakeholders, and views expressed by participants in the July 28, 2004 public meeting suggest that government could pursue one or more of the following strategies:

- play a role in coordinating and supporting the development of IPv6 standards, protocols, and conformance;
- be an active participant in identifying and facilitating solutions for technological and interoperability issues; and
- stimulate adoption as a major consumer of IPv6 products and services when it is in the best interest of the individual government agencies.

However, industry should continue to take the lead in developing the IPv6 standards architecture, with coordination support and participation from government. Similarly, industry consortia and academic institutions should take the lead in conformance testing and development of interoperability solutions to support implementation, with support and participation from government. Finally, government has an important role to play as a consumer of IPv6 products and services and, therefore, must carefully evaluate the security and economic factors affecting adoption and assimilation of the new technology into federal IT systems. Private-sector decisions to purchase IPv6 products and services should be market driven, without influence from the federal government.

This section addresses the circumstances that could warrant government action to stimulate deployment of IPv6 in the United States. Market failures are commonly cited as one of the primary motives for government involvement in technology development and deployment. Technological market failure refers to a condition under which either the producers and/or users of a technology underinvest relative to society's optimal level of investment. Infratechnology research to support standardization, development of interoperability solutions, and conformance testing are all classic examples of where private returns on investment are not only less than social returns, but are below minimum private sector rates of return (so-called "hurdle rates"). In such cases, the needed infratechnologies and related services are commonly supported by some joint industry-government research and development (RandD) and technology transfer activities.

The levels of investment in such technical infrastructure will affect the potential realization of benefits from IPv6. Sufficient levels of investment are needed to minimize interoperability problems and to realize the positive network externalities generated by IPv6. [217] Because network externalities can be difficult for the private sector to appropriate, the public sector frequently supports investment in infratechnologies, such as interoperability protocols, conformance testing, and certification mechanisms, which reduce adoption costs and integrate market segments.

The timing of investments will also affect the costs and benefits of adopting IPv6. Accelerating deployment beyond normal equipment/software replacement life cycles will increase transition and replacement costs. Alternatively, lagging behind other nations in the deployment of technologies such as IPv6 may have competitiveness implications if foreign countries can capture first-mover advantages, although as discussed above, first-mover advantages do not appear to be a significant concern with respect to IPv6 at this time.

Thus, government can affect market evolution through its role as a major consumer of IPv6 products and services by stimulating private-sector investment. Its purchases for internal government use have the potential to influence the timing of IPv6 deployment by providing initial markets of sufficient size to enable learning curve progression by suppliers and to create product/service performance data for potential private sector consumers.

5.1. Potential Market Failures and Underinvestment in IPv6

The premise that markets may "fail" to invest in socially optimal amounts of RandD or new technologies has long been accepted by economists and is now being embraced by policy makers. [218] Much of the technological market failure literature focuses on underinvestment in innovation or in the creation or production of RandD-derived technology. However, these economic arguments are also applicable to the purchase and use of the technology that results from RandD.

5.1.1. Potential IPv6 Market Barriers and Underinvestment

Broadly speaking, underinvestment occurs because conditions exist that prevent firms from fully realizing or appropriating the benefits created by their investments, thereby causing firms to view prospective investments in new technologies as having expected rates of return below the firm's minimum acceptable rate of return (hurdle rate). Although firms may recognize that there are spillover benefits to other markets or consumers, they are likely to ignore or heavily discount these benefits because they generally do not translate into increased profits for the investing firm. Moreover, research to support development of interoperability solutions, conformance testing, and other infratechnologies that become the basis of standards are all paradigmatic examples of cases where private returns to investment can be less than both social returns and private hurdle rates. As a result, those activities are frequently supported by government activities. [219]

Some uncertainty exists among U.S. ISPs and the software community concerning the likelihood that the private returns from IPv6 deployment and its subsequent market opportunities will justify the costs associated with the transition. [220] These concerns, however, are attributable less to appropriability issues and more to (1) uncertainties over users' willingness to pay for IPv6 products and services, and (2) the negative effect of relatively high present value assigned to the up-front, and potentially substantial, transition costs.

5.1.2. Timing of Investment

In apparent contradiction to this assessment, most commenters see no need for government intervention and expect market forces to generate sufficient returns to drive efficient development and deployment of IPv6 over time. [221] A partial explanation may be that the transition technologies being developed and implemented by the IETF are viewed as ensuring that initially small negative network externalities will not hinder the adoption of IPv6. The IETF's objective is for IPv6 systems, devices, and products to be able to interoperate with IPv4 networks and devices, thereby avoiding the potential disincentive to first movers attributable to negative economic incentives flowing from low network externalities. [222]

Other commenters assert that because the research needed to develop and deploy IPv6 may exhibit characteristics of a "public good," a continuing need exists for government support. [223] Appropriability issues are most likely to occur as part of the development of generic infrastructure and applications technologies and infratechnologies needed to enable IPv6. On average, early actions or market interventions by government are likely to have the greatest impact on IPv6 deployment. One commenter notes that government activities that take place over the initial three years of IPv6 development and deployment may have significant long-term returns for both private (monetary) and public (economic growth) interests. [224]

In general, the closer RandD activities move toward commercialization, the less government should be involved. Market forces should be allowed to drive research for product and service development, where a greater likelihood exists that firms will be able to appropriate adequate returns and where innovators are more likely to face risk and reward conditions compatible with private-sector investment criteria. [225]

5.1.3. Concerns Related to the Chicken-or-Egg Dilemma

When complementary products or services are needed to realize the benefits from a new technology, the potential for a chicken-or-egg dilemma arises. One example of this phenomenon is the interrelationship between the adoption of high definition television (HDTV) sets and the availability of high-definition program content. In such cases, increased deployment of one of the component technologies generates externalities that increase the benefits to be derived from the adoption of the complementary technologies.

Similarly, for IPv6, the chicken-or-egg dilemma can be defined as the presence of disincentives for investment in supporting infrastructure until applications are deployed, contrasted with disincentives for investment in applications until supporting infrastructure is in place. If equipment manufacturers and software manufacturers are reluctant to make the first-mover investments until complementary IPv6 infratechnologies/standards are in place, an investment barrier could exist for some time.

Several commenters portrayed the chicken-or-egg issue as one in which demand is not currently high enough to push vendors and ISPs to deploy IPv6 products and services, while uncertainty exists on the part of potential buyers of those products and services regarding the nature, degree, and timeliness of IPv6 benefits. [226] Users are often initially risk averse with respect to potential innovations, however, thereby placing the onus on first movers to demonstrate the new technology's potential. These first movers can be discouraged by a costly and incomplete infrastructure, including standards.

Commenters suggested that government could help resolve this chicken-or-egg dilemma by providing information on the current status of IPv6 infrastructure and conformance testing requirements. For example, infrastructure issues, such as the prevalence of NAT boxes and fear of interdependence between IPv6 applications and ISP routing services, are among the reasons why some networks are not testing and developing IPv6 applications. [227] Better information and access to transition tools could help.

Most commenters, however, indicated that the chicken-or-egg issue is not a serious problem, suggesting that markets are pushing IPv6 development and deployment in an appropriate time frame. They stated that transition mechanisms were designed specifically to circumvent the problem of having to "throw a switch," and noted ongoing development activities resulting from market demand. [228]

A principal reason for this majority viewpoint is that IPv6 is not a totally new infrastructure. IPv6 and IPv4 are not exclusively different alternatives in that most benefits associated with IPv6 can also be realized by an enhanced IPv4 system (however, at potentially greater costs). For this reason, IPv6 will likely be deployed over time, and to differing degrees, by various stakeholder groups, as opposed to a mass and "instant" migration. Because IPv6 and IPv4 are designed to be interoperable during the transition period, moreover, this mitigates any potential chicken-or-egg dilemma.

The issue of demand by users, mentioned above, can be stated in terms of uncertainty over users' willingness to pay for IPv6-enabled products.

Consumers' valuation of products and services, however, is typically not a market failure issue. For a problem to exist, barriers to market growth, in particular market aggregation, must be demonstrated. As noted above, large markets based on a new standard do not necessarily materialize instantly. Small market segments can appear that do not initially benefit from significant externalities. In fact, aggregation to larger markets typically occurs over time.

Nevertheless, segmentation, especially if accompanied by interoperability problems across segments, can inhibit the aggregation process. This issue must be monitored and addressed as warranted because global competition shortens life cycles and protracted barriers to penetration in domestic markets can (as discussed earlier) disadvantage domestic firms. The IETF transition strategy is designed to avoid such a situation by allowing initially small IPv6 markets to coexist (interoperate) with IPv4 applications, thereby avoiding an all-or-nothing transition. Nevertheless, coexistence does not guarantee market agglomeration for IPv6 applications.

In summary, the chicken-or-egg dilemma is probably not a serious concern with respect to the adoption of IPv6. The prevailing view seems to be that the drivers for IPv6 technologies will be consumer and enterprise applications that require IPv6 or that are impractical and more costly to implement via IPv4. Once these technologies materialize, ISPs should be able to rapidly enable hardware (which should already be IPv6 capable). Assuming that the initial markets are sufficiently large to enable at least modest network externalities and that adequate interoperability is provided, users will likely move quickly to adopt IPv6 software applications. [229]

5.1.4. Standards, Protocols, and Conformance Issues

The enabling of IPv6 technology cannot occur in the absence of standards and protocols that facilitate the coordination of the technologies along the supply chain and across different suppliers. Standards are a classic example of a public good because they represent a type of infrastructure where spillovers are not only socially desirable but necessary (by definition, a standard implies common, nonrivalrous use). In general, the Internet, by its very nature, is an open system, and the value of IP standards increases with the free flow of information. As a result, government has and will continue to have a role in how the Internet and related technologies evolve.

IPv6 development has been the subject of public and private research for many years, with the majority of findings residing in the public domain.

However, many issues still must be addressed with respect to both infrastructure and applications. Because network externalities generated by nonproduct standards cannot be appropriated, private incentives to participate in the standards development process are typically well below socially optimal benefits and lead to suboptimal levels of participation. [230] Private returns alone are not likely to provide sufficient motivation to stimulate investments in these areas. [231] For this reason, the public sector has a stake in the IPv6 standards development process, program coordination, infratechnology development, and information dissemination. As noted above, government agencies are in a unique position to promote collaborative processes.

Specifically, government can participate with the private sector and other entities in implementing IPv6 through activities such as infratechnology development and conformance testing for the standards based on these infratechnologies. [232] For example, most respondents to the RFC indicated that government could continue and even expand its coordination and funding of research to develop solutions to interoperability problems. Protocols, conformance testing methods, and roadmap processes are critical for IPv6 systems developers and implementers. Moreover, respondents proposed that the U.S. government could support IPv6 research into interoperability with existing IPv4 systems [233] in addition to coordinating trials and tests of new IPv6-enabled devices—routers, hosts, PDAs, etc. Government could support both the harmonization of standards and interoperability testing activities, such as those currently being developed and performed by the University of New Hampshire, the TAHI project, and the European Telecommunications Standards Institute (ETSI). [234]

5.2. Potential Roles for Government Involvement in IPv6

The evidence gathered by the Task Force indicates a general consensus among various stakeholders that market forces should be allowed to drive the private sector transition from IPv4 to IPv6. No stakeholder indicated that significant market impediments exist for the adoption of IPv6; thus, all stakeholders believed that the federal government should refrain from actions that would significantly interfere with market forces. As MCI points out, "[a]lthough the deployment of IPv6 has occurred more slowly than was anticipated when the IETF began work on IPv6, there is no evidence of a market failure warranting government intervention. To a great extent, the current pace of IPv6 deployment reflects the normal weighing of benefits and costs that is associated with any technology deployment." [235]

Many respondents referenced the GOSIP mandate and indicated that widespread concern and a lack of confidence remained within the computer networking community regarding government-led standardization activities. [236] One expert suggested that considering the negative impact of the GOSIP initiative, government should not consider a mandate for IPv6, but rather contribute to the development and deployment of IPv6 by facilitating testing and other collaborative efforts. [237] Commenting parties generally agreed that a government mandate for IPv6 deployment by industry is not appropriate at this time. [238]

However, most respondents also emphasized the public good nature of IPv6 and suggested that the public sector should foster development and deployment. This was frequently linked to concerns that the United States is lagging behind in developing and deploying IPv6 and that U.S. competitiveness and IT leadership will suffer without appropriate government activity.

In addition to national competitiveness, security issues were also cited as a motivating factor for government involvement in IPv6. Although there was no agreement on whether IPv6 would lead to security improvements, the public good nature of Internet security in general was acknowledged along with concerns regarding the maintenance of security during the transition to IPv6. [239] For example, commenters suggested that both government and the private sector need to work on trust relationships and key management (e.g., PKI development). [240]

One participant at the July 2004 public meeting coined the acronym "RUDE" to describe the sorts of government activities that could support the development and deployment of IPv6 in the United States:

- Research it independently or in collaboration with interested private-sector stakeholders;
- Use it in government communications networks;
- Defend the ability of U.S. firms to compete fully and fairly in global markets for IPv6 products, networks, and services; and
- Encourage IPv6 use by disseminating information inside and outside of government. [241]

5.2.1. Government Support for RandD

Respondents suggested the government should support certain types of RandD activities. Several government organizations that perform Internet-related testing and/or research were mentioned: NIST, the National Science Foundation (NSF); the Department of Energy (DOE); National Aeronautics and Space Administration (NASA), the Advanced Research Projects Agency/Defense Advanced Research Projects Agency (ARPA/DARPA), and the Department of Homeland Security (DHS). It was stated that organizations such as NIST and NTIA are ideally positioned to help foster and facilitate government collaboration with universities and industry. [242]

To ensure that IPv6-enabled services are deployed in a timely manner, the government could work to build the necessary base of skilled human resources in order to sustain the research effort and to encourage the acceleration of standards and specifications work. Suggestions for specific research focus areas include interoperability, security, and transition mechanisms. Additionally, the government might support the development of new applications and possibly initiate test beds similar to Moonv6, as appropriate to meet the needs of its agencies. Government funding for advanced test bed deployment could be made available and advertised appropriately. [243]

Some of the areas that commenters identified for further research include the following: [244]

- testing of IPv6's interoperability with existing IPv4 systems;
- techniques to improve the performance and efficiency of IPv6 for key applications such as VoIP;
- mobile IPv6 routing;
- routing limitations in which the cost of a multihomed site is not completely borne by that site, but rather by the network as a whole;
- performance in dual IPv4/IPv6 environments;
- security in dual-stack environments;
- intrusion detection techniques for IPv6, including implications for changes in the use of tunneling and NATs;
- privacy implications of IPv6;
- PKI scalability and trust models; and
- secure Border Gateway Protocol (BGP) implications.

5.2.2. Government as a Consumer

Most commenters stated that government intervention to direct the markets for IPv6 products and services would be unwarranted and potentially harmful. Nevertheless, all respondents indicated that government has an important role to play as a major consumer of IPv6 products and services. From this perspective, federal agencies could play a significant role as early adopters of IPv6. [245] In fact, some commenters suggested that other federal government agencies should follow the DoD's lead and consider deploying IPv6. [246] Most commenters, however, asserted that government agencies should adopt IPv6 only when such adoption meets agency needs. [247] They also recommended against requiring state and local governments to establish specific IPv6 deployment schedules. [248] The federal government, however, could encourage its own networks to formulate transition plans and begin implementing IPv6 as soon as practical.

5.2.3. Information Dissemination

The federal government has an important role in disseminating information and providing training support to promote and lower the cost of IPv6 deployment. The government can help to ensure that all stakeholders are aware of the benefits and costs of IPv6 and disseminate information to individual companies to promote the development of cost-effective transition strategies. [249] Government could engage in awareness campaigns and provide training resources to disseminate information on IPv6

A key component of any company's transition strategy will be staff training and education. Training and education are likely to be one of the greatest cost components associated with adopting IPv6. Not only will existing staff need to be retrained, but many new graduates will also need additional specific training because universities are not producing sufficient numbers of IPv6-aware network engineers. [250] Cisco Systems suggests that until the IPv6 "educated base" is expanded, that is, until networking students learn about IPv6 technology, private-sector training costs will be very large. Other commenters agree and suggested that government involvement could offset some of this cost. [251]

Government could continue, and possibly expand, its collaborations with universities to provide centers of learning for IPv6, which could include seminars, workshops, and training classes to support local businesses. Classes focused on teaching the business community the technical specifics of IPv6 implementation (e.g., transition techniques and required hardware and software upgrades/replacements) and use (e.g., applications and tools) have the potential to lower the cost of and accelerate the deployment of IPv6.

Additionally, the government could increase its participation in groups such as the IETF to help develop "best current practices" to be used in these education programs or merely posted for use by government agencies and U.S. companies. [252] The government could also create and maintain a library of IPv6 information and resources that interested parties can access. [253] The NAv6TF further suggests that the government encourage the integration of IPv6 through the creation of a favorable, stable, and government-supported program to avoid the development of fragmented approaches. [254] In general, many commenters agreed that, by actively supporting training opportunities and promotional activities, government could help lower the cost of IPv6 deployment. [255]

Chapter 6

FINDINGS

GENERAL

The Task Force concludes that the United States and other economies are in the early stages of IPv6 adoption and deployment. As such, many uncertainties exist with respect to the benefits and costs of prospective market applications and, therefore, the benefits and costs of alternative transition scenarios. Nevertheless, a consensus exists with respect to the likely long-term importance of IPv6 adoption. At this time, most of the stakeholders participating in the Task Force's activities believe that the current market-driven adoption of IPv6 by the private sector is proceeding at a reasonable pace and that the instituted transition mechanisms will enable efficient migration at acceptable cost. The push for adoption in other countries, however, could potentially change this situation, and the complexity of the infrastructure necessary to effect the transition from IPv4 to IPv6 may require additional support. Thus, a number of technology and economic policy issues need to be examined regularly in order to determine, over time, what support, if any, may be needed for the growing IPv6 activities by industry and by federal, state, and local governments.

In this context, the Task Force has reached the following findings:

1. IPv6 is a complex standard consisting of a suite of protocols, definitions, transition mechanisms, and operational procedures. These protocols are at varying stages of maturity, with varying scopes of applicability and varying subsets of mandatory/recommended/discretionary implementation options. In the near term, the net benefits of IPv6 compared with IPv4 will vary

among organizations and deployment scenarios, both domestically and internationally. Still, the Task Force recognizes the long-term benefits of an evolution to a protocol with a significantly larger address space than IPv4.

2. A collection of techniques (e.g., NATs) have been developed and deployed in recent years to accommodate the growing demand for IPv4 addresses, but these "fixes" impose operational inefficiencies and costs. If, as a many observers anticipate, large-scale demand for new, address-intensive applications such as mobile communications, remote monitoring, and consumer Internet-TV emerge, the continued viability of such techniques comes into question.
3. IPv6 stakeholders can be organized into four major groups:
   - Infrastructure (Hardware and Software) Vendors
   - Application Vendors
   - Internet Service Providers (ISPs)
   - Internet Users

   The potential benefits, costs, and risks associated with IPv6 adoption can vary significantly across this range of stakeholders. Any analysis of such issues should, therefore, be specific to each of these groups.
4. The Task Force recognizes that the complexity involved in IPv6 adoption and use also varies greatly with specific deployment scenarios; ranging from so-called "isolated greenfield" implementations (primarily new private networks) to transitioning the Internet (existing and public networks), which is a large and complex problem. In addition, the scope of IPv6 adoption can vary greatly within a network, so careful consideration must be given to which network devices, applications, management, and control functions are to be affected.
5. Based on the above findings, the Task Force concludes that both public- and private-sector users of networked information technology should begin planning for the emergence of IPv6 technologies and analyze requirements and appropriate schedules for adoption. In the near term, in order to ensure the security and stability of both new IPv6-enabled IT systems and the existing systems with which they must interoperate, the Task Force stresses that careful planning, development, and evaluation should be undertaken for the forthcoming dual-standard environment. Within federal networks, the identified need to expedite IPv6 planning and

analysis is consistent with other recent government studies [256] and evolving policies. [257]

6. Recognizing that several crucial aspects of IPv6 remain to be specified and that all elements of the technical basis for the standard need significant additional test and evaluation experience, the Task Force notes that the federal government will need to commit new resources and to work collaboratively with other public and private sector entities to address these outstanding research, development, and testing issues. Given the scope and importance of these issues, identification of a specific entity to coordinate these activities within the federal government and among similar international efforts should be considered.

ECONOMIC GROWTH AND COMPETITIVE IMPACTS

The global scope of the Internet means that both domestic private investment and the standards infrastructure supporting the Internet must evolve in a timely manner. That evolution will be complex because of the multiple industries involved in the delivery of Internet infrastructure and the myriad of existing and emerging services that depend upon it. Although the Task Force concurs with the general view that the transition to IPv6 is occurring at an acceptable pace, some industries in the Internet supply chain are migrating to the new protocol at faster rates than are others. Therefore, a number of trends and potential barriers must be continually monitored and assessed.

Major portions of the Internet infrastructure hardware and software markets appear to be IPv6 "capable" already, and over the next four or five years, the vast majority of network hardware, operating systems, and network-enabled software packages (e.g., databases, email) will be sold with IPv6 capabilities. This capability is not actually "turned on," however. In the next few years, users will begin to "enable" or "turn on" this capability in operating systems, or they will purchase operating systems with IPv6 "on by default." In fact, the majority of Linux-based operating systems are IPv6 enabled today, and the next version of Windows, due out in 2007, will likely be IPv6 enabled by default. As operating systems become enabled and early adopters provide "lessons learned," respondents predict that users will start to enable routers, followed finally by applications.

Applications are the key driver because they will create demand for the aforementioned categories of IPv6 infrastructure. Application vendors are moving toward IPv6 at a much slower pace than are infrastructure vendors, however. Many application developers have been testing IPv6 and planning to integrate IPv6 into their products, although very few have actually begun selling IPv6-capable products, at least in the United States. Many of these vendors are indicating that they plan to release IPv6-capable products as early as 2007.

Many ISPs that do not also provide Internet backbone facilities are not offering IPv6 connectivity because they do not want to incur costs without a reasonably certain return on investment. Consequently, although numerous ISPs are currently engaged in testing activities and may offer limited IPv6 services, they appear to be waiting for a significant number of mainstream customers to request IPv6 connectivity. At that point, those ISPs indicate that they will be prepared to provide service in six months to one year. Like users, however, ISPs do not intend to offer IPv6 service until major hardware and software network components are in place.

More generally, emerging and future address-intensive, peer-to-peer Internet applications will exhibit an iterative relationship with the supporting infrastructure. That is, the availability of a higher capacity and more efficient standards infrastructure leverages private-sector innovation, which, in turn, increases the use of and demand for improvements in the supporting infrastructure. Thus, monitoring the evolution of the "chicken-or-egg" relationship between infrastructure and innovation is important for long-term domestic economic growth policy and implies an optimum balance between public and private investment in technology-based industries. Most stakeholders in the U.S. believe that IETF-fashioned transition strategies will allow fast market response at reasonable cost to the emergence of demand for IPv6-dependent applications.

Over time, the net benefits of IPv6 will increase for all industries using the Internet, but currently, nations competing with the United States have a greater incentive to migrate to IPv6 due to perceived limitations in IPv4 address space. That fact is a two-edged sword. On the one hand, the vast installed base of IPv4 infrastructure and applications buys time with respect to transition decisions. On the other hand, a large installed base can act as a barrier to change from IPv4 to IPv6 because of the sunk costs and the fact that the IPv4 infrastructure provides an acceptable level of service and functionality for most users.

Because the rest of the world is clearly migrating toward IPv6, a long-term competitiveness issue faces the U.S. economy, namely, the potential to develop and deploy more advanced Internet services that either require IPv6 or run much more efficiently on it. Unfortunately, the rate and scope of market penetration by these new Internet services are difficult to predict. As they become more prevalent globally, the burden on U.S. companies that still emphasize IPv4 while trying to also migrate to IPv6 applications will steadily increase. [258]

Conversely, premature migration to a new generation standard with the high transition costs typical of complex standards (such as the Internet Protocol) can impose large short-term and even medium-term costs on domestic firms

COSTS

The costs of transition will be incurred unevenly across the industries and user groups that comprise the Internet supply chain. The timing of these costs and their distribution across stakeholder groups will be affected by the appearance of IPv6-specific applications and the degree to which industry and government efficiently execute industry-led transition strategies.

For individual organizations within each user group—corporate, institutional, government, and individuals—the transition costs will vary widely. For example, independent users, comprised of home users and small businesses, will likely incur virtually no cost to move to IPv6 as they would gain IPv6 enablement over time without additional testing and installation costs. [259]

Medium-sized businesses, on the other hand, will likely incur the largest relative increase in IT spending to transition to IPv6. The majority of these costs will be related to the core networking operations and staff, the size of which does not increase proportionally to the size of an organization. The magnitude of costs for medium-sized businesses will be slightly less than large organizations, but their annual revenues are significantly lower. Therefore, the costs for medium-sized businesses relative to sales will be much higher.

Industry indicates that over the next four or five years the vast majority of network hardware, operating systems, and network-enabled software packages (e.g., databases, email, etc.) will be sold with IPv6 capabilities as users upgrade or replace worn out hardware and software. As a result, users may not incur significant additional hardware/software costs to acquire IPv6-capable IT systems. However, having the capability to run IPv6-based applications is significantly different from having access to and running actual applications. To do so will require the emergence of applications and the "turning on" or "enabling" of the hardware and software. This will require re-training of IT staff. Thus, the Task Force's research and analysis indicate that labor (training) costs will constitute the majority of the total extraordinary costs of upgrading to IPv6 for users.

BENEFITS

As a technical matter, IPv6 has advantages over IPv4. Over time, the technical advantages of the new protocol will likely produce several types of benefits. There are, however, significant disagreements among stakeholders about the timing and magnitude of those potential benefits, as well as their distribution among providers and users.

The most frequently cited infrastructure benefit from the adoption of IPv6 is a vast increase in available addresses for people and machines that need to be connected. Demand for such addresses will likely increase as more and more of the world's population requests Internet access. The situation may become critical if the projected markets emerge for in-home devices (e.g., "smart appliances," entertainment systems, voice/video over IP) that need to be accessible from outside the home via the Internet. Although there is considerable disagreement about whether, to what extent, and at what pace, such demand will develop, IPv6 would provide the address space to accommodate any level of demand which emerges.

Emerging market applications, especially devices that are globally addressable so that they can be remotely accessed and controlled via the Internet, represent a potentially important application of IPv6 addresses. Further, automobile components or subsystems, refrigerators, cameras, home computers, and other home appliances could be assigned IP addresses, linked together on home networks, and connected to the Internet. Home owners could control such devices remotely, and automobile and appliance manufacturers, for example, could offer remote service and support packages. Wireless sensor networks and machine-to-machine communications will eventually lead to the proliferation of devices that will connect to the Internet.

Additional benefits of remote access are the potential increased life expectancies of large ticket items such as automobiles and appliances (durable goods) and an associated decrease in service/repair costs. For example, RTI estimated that a one percent increase in life expectancy and one percent decrease in service costs for automobiles and appliances would yield approximately $3 billion dollars in economic benefits.

Network efficiency benefits flowing from adoption of IPv6 could also be significant. Many of the benefits hinge on removing and/or changing the management of NATs, firewalls, and middleboxes, because they currently disrupt certain types of end-to-end connections. A NAT-enabled firewall presents a small number of public addresses to the Internet and, therefore, conserves limited address capacity (a problem under IPv4), while using private IP addresses for all the personal computers behind it. Participating stakeholders indicated that application vendors allocate significant labor resources to design or redesign their products so that they will work through NAT boxes. Some experts have stated that this work could stifle innovation by diverting time away from other infrastructure and application RandD activities and by increasing the complexity of new applications.

SECURITY IMPLICATIONS

Over the long term, adoption and use of IPv6 by government, the private sector, and the Internet as a whole may produce security benefits. In the short term, implementation on any new communications protocol, such as IPv6, will likely increase security threats to networks and users. The greatest potential security benefits of IPv6, moreover, appear to depend on the development and implementation of security mechanisms and paradigms significantly different than those commonly employed in today's networks and largely independent of the particular Internet protocol (e.g., IPv6 or IPv4). Additionally, the transition mechanisms that will be employed during the lengthy migration from IPv4 to IPv6 will likely present their own security concerns and challenges.

Effective and secure migration to IPv6 will require careful testing and evaluation, deployment guidance and standards, and development of IPv6-aware security hardware, policies, and processes. Adoption of IPv6 may also necessitate the replacement of existing perimeter security architectures with end-to-end architectures. That will require research and development expenditures for new security management technologies and mechanisms.

Consequently, the potential security benefits of IPv6 in the longer term must be balanced against (1) what might be considerable development costs to complete the design and development of these new models, (2) potential increased risks entailed by deploying such models incrementally in existing operational networks, and (3) the ability to deploy security improvements (such as IPsec) without deploying IPv6. In the near- to mid-term, carefully integrated security planning, IPv6-specific security development, and security testing should precede any organization's decision to deploy new IPv6 technologies operationally so as to ensure the security and stability of both the new IPv6 resources and the existing resources that they may interact with. Failure to do so could easily result in degrading the security posture of the organization's existing IT systems.

DEPLOYMENT STRATEGIES/OPTIONS

The Task Force believes that, consistent with existing laws and within current resources, the federal government has four major roles with respect to deployment of IPv6:

- continue to monitor and analyze technological and market trends in global IPv6 infrastructure and applications;
- conduct research on IPv6 infratechnologies and facilitate industry standardization processes;
- support industry with performance/behavior test methods and test beds, as needed; and
- deploy and enable IPv6 to meet internal government IT needs, after adequate planning.

Industry expressed a range of views on government roles in facilitating deployment of IPv6. In general, infrastructure vendors and users were more enthusiastic about government involvement than were application vendors and ISPs. Moreover, infrastructure vendors and users differed in the type of activities and technical areas where they believed government should be involved. Additionally, most stakeholders mentioned government research and test beds related to development of scalable end-to-end security models and quality of service mechanisms. Regarding adoption, many stakeholders specifically suggested that government support in standards and protocol development, along with compliance and interoperability testing, should be provided through existing industry standards bodies such as the IETF and existing test beds such as Moonv6.

With respect to procurement, the federal government is a major market for IT systems, including Internet applications. It can thus provide an initial market of substantial size, which will both demonstrate to the rest of the economy the value of IPv6 applications and provide data on the most cost-effective strategies for transitioning to the new protocol.

Any federal government IPv6 initiative, however, must include careful planning and both procurement and deployment strategies to be effective (the previous experiment with federal procurement policy toward Internet protocols, GOSIP, only mandated procurement and, as a result, failed). Moreover, given that industry has led efforts to date on IPv6 research and development, standardization, and deployment, a government procurement and deployment policy will only be successful if government coordinates with industry and provides internal technical expertise to assist government agencies to develop and implement transition strategies.

APPENDIX A

HYPOTHETICAL CASE STUDY: ENTERPRISE ADOPTION OF IPV6

The costs associated with an enterprise adoption of IPv6 can best be illustrated through a hypothetical case study. [260] Company A, a medium-to-large enterprise with an IPv4-only corporate network, determines that to contact Company B via an IPv6 connection, Company A needs to begin migrating its network to IPv6. This transition will cause Company A to incur costs for hardware, software, labor, as well as other costs that may arise from unforeseen or unpredictable security threats and other hurdles (e.g., interoperability).

Company A's network infrastructure, combined with its present and desired future applications strategies, will determine the appropriate transition process and costs. For the purposes of this case study, we assume that Company A has eight core routers, 150 distribution switches, and four firewalls, all with varying individual costs. The primary applications that the company uses would need to be IPv6-capable, including limited video conferencing, some streaming video, and a company-wide inventory database. Company A has three full-time network specialists and allocates approximately $2,500 per year per employee on training. Table A-1 provides a breakdown of the infrastructure owned by Company A and its annual spending on IT staff and training.

Table A-1. Existing Infrastructure Components and Annual Labor Expenses for Hypothetical Company A

Network Component/Costs	Number of Units	Average likely Cost (per unit)	Total Cost
Router	8	$15,000	$120,000
Distribution Switches	150	$10,000	$1,500,000
Firewall	4	$1,500	$6,000
Network Specialist (1 Full Time Equivalent (FTE))	3	$55,000	$165,000/year
Training	3	$2,500	$7,500/year
TOTAL			$1,798,500

Source: RTI Networking Staff

In order to get immediate connection capabilities, Company A plans to establish a limited IPv6 network over a 6- to 12-month period; however, the majority of costs will be spread out over a transition period lasting at least several years. In the most likely scenario, Company A will follow a migration path that gradually increases the number of applications running IPv6 and the ability of its network to handle more IPv6 traffic. Table A-2 compares the costs as Company A progresses through the various stages of its migration strategy.

In Phase 1, Company A will transition from an IPv4-only network to an IPv4 network with IPv6 tunneling. [261] It will employ tunneling primarily to allow IPv6 communication with outside organizations and networks at a low cost; thus, they will employ host-to-host tunneling using a tunnel broker. By reconfiguring the network for tunneling and running dual-stack operating systems on hosts, Company A would provide IPv6 connectivity for a limited subset of the company's hosts as a pilot group. Connectivity will later be extended to the entire corporate network and user base.

The extent of the costs associated with this first phase of migration will rely heavily on the presence of IPv6 capabilities within the network and host hardware and software. [262] After assessing hardware and software capabilities, Company A will need to develop a plan for how and when to incorporate IPv6 into its network.

This effort will involve contributions not only from IT administrators, but also from company leaders and/or any Internet users who can communicate the desire to have certain IPv6 capabilities. Such a process should take several months and could be quite costly in terms of labor effort.

Table A-2. Transition Phases and Associated Costs

Transition Phases	Relative Estimated Size of Cost	Costs			
		Hardware	Software	Labor	Other
Phase 1 (Minimal IPv6 using tunneling in a subset of the network)	Medium	Upgrading/ Eplacing Backbone routers; replacing firewalls	Upgrading/ replacing any software that supports major network components	Existing IT personnel must be trained; new personnel may need to be hired to help install and run a dualprotocol network and to address new/additional security concerns	Scheduled downtime
Phase 2 [a] (Substantial IPv6 using a dual-stack network)	Large	Upgrading/ replacing remaining routers and all other networking hardware	Upgrading/ replacing all applications to be IPv6 capable	More IT training and network administration time/effort will be required before, during and after the installation; users might need to be trained to use new applications	More scheduled downtime; unexpected equipment and service outages; security threat effects
Phase 3 [b] (Native IPv6 with IPv4 translation and/or limited dual-stack)	Small/ Medium	Upgrading/ replacing gateways and other devices to perform translation	Depending on the translation mechanism, new software may be required	Time/effort to install and maintain translation devices; training and support for users running only IPv6 applications	Interoperability issues with external Internet users/networks [c]
Phase 4 (Native IPv6 only)	Small	None	None	Time/effort to remove translation devices and software	Potential loss of business

RTI estimates based on RFC responses and discussions with industry stakeholders.

[a] The costs described in Phase 2 assume that Phase 1 has been completed.

[b] The costs described in Phase 3 assume that Phase 2 has been completed. Additionally, several experts have noted that this step will be skipped in most cases.

[c] Security threats will continue but most likely at a reduced cost since IPv6 intrusions will be better understood.

Addressing specific expenditures, we note that Phase 1 equipment costs will include upgrading/replacing one or more routers to allow IPv6 tunneling and replacing firewalls and intrusion detection system (IDS) equipment for security. Unless Company A has an urgent need to gain IPv6 connectivity, it will incur these costs during a routine three- to five-year equipment upgrade cycle. Thus, a "size of cost" estimate does not include hardware and software costs. Because most computer operating systems currently support IPv6 (e.g., Windows and Linux), software costs for a pilot group of IPv6 users will be limited to any upgrades of applications to be used specifically with IPv6.

Labor and training costs will be a large part of this initial migration phase. Existing IT personnel must be trained to support IPv6. New personnel may be hired to assist with the operational overhead of installing IPv6, running two Internet protocols on a network, and addressing potential security concerns commonly associated with any major IT transition. Scheduled downtime and unexpected outages of equipment and services related to upgrades will result in additional costs.

As Company A decides to enable more internal Internet hosts to use IPv6, it will likely begin Phase 2 of its migration by integrating dual-stack capabilities into network routers that would allow more IPv6 messages to be sent and received, and would make such communication more efficient. Although Windows-based hosts could use Microsoft's Teredo to send IPv6 messages with no changes to existing routers, [263] companies interested in transitioning to IPv6 will likely enable dual-stack capabilities in their network routers, as well as on most or all of their network and IT infrastructure while maintaining normal IPv4 operation.

Phase 2 will involve configuring dual-stack routers and running IPv4 and IPv6 simultaneously on most network equipment and hosts. Hardware not upgraded to IPv6 in Phase 1 will be upgraded during this phase. However, the majority of the costs will come from software upgrades and associated labor costs necessary to roll out new IPv6 services and applications to a large number of corporate users. [264] Training costs will also be incurred because these users need to be trained on new applications. Security issues will also require labor expenditures and, possibly, additional hardware and software.

In Phase 3 of Company A's migration plan, it will use IPv6 predominantly for network transmission, and use either dual-stack capable subnetworks or IPv6-to-IPv4 translation to interact with internal and external IPv4 networks. The decision to move from Phase 2 to Phase 3 will turn on cost savings – whether the costs of network support for IPv4 exceed the costs of supporting IPv6. Estimated to be many years away, Phase 3 will most likely involve employing an IPv6 network with remaining "pockets" of IPv4 within the company. Equipment continuing to run IPv4 even after this phase may include legacy information pieces, such as mainframes and databases that are too expensive to upgrade during Phase 3. The only likely equipment costs are gateways and other devices if IPv4/IPv6 translation is needed. Labor costs may be incurred for planning, testing, and moving to native IPv6, as well for the installation and maintenance of these translation devices. Additional labor costs may come from supporting a large base of users now running IPv6 natively and the associated issues that may arise.

Lastly, as IPv4 traffic becomes less common, Company A will decide not to support translation devices. In Phase 4, any networks or hosts still operating on IPv4 stacks will have to have dual-stack capabilities or translation devices to communicate with IPv6-only hosts or networks.

APPENDIX B

I. RFC COMMENTERS

- Alcatel North America, Inc.
- BellSouth
- Cisco Systems, Inc.
- Gordon Cook, The Cook Report on Internet Protocol Technology, Economics and Policy
- Michael Dillon
- Electronic Privacy Information Center
- General Service Administration (GSA) Federal Technology Service
- Tony Hain
- Geoff Huston, Asia Pacific Network Information Centre
- Internet Security Alliance
- Internet2
- Lockheed Martin Corporation • Microsoft Corporation
- Motorola, Inc.
- Network Conceptions LLC
- North American IPv6 Task Force
- NTT/Verio
- Qwest Communications International, Inc.
- Sprint Corporation
- VeriSign, Inc.
- WorldCom, Inc. d/b/a/ MCI

II. PUBLIC MEETING PANELISTS

- Stan Barber, Vice President, Engineering Operations, Verio
- Jim Bound, Chairman, North American IPv6 Task Force
- Mark Desautels, Vice President, Wireless Internet Development, CTIA
- Dr. Paul Francis, Associate Professor, Cornell University
- Tony Hain, Senior Technical Leader, Cisco
- Henry Kafka, Vice President, Architecture and Emerging Technologies, BellSouth
- Marilyn Kraus, Technical Advisor, Office of Chief Information Officer, U.S. Department of Defense
- Dr. Latif Ladid, President, IPv6 Forum
- Dr. Paul Liao, Vice President and Chief Technology Officer, Panasonic
- Preston Marshall, Program Manager, Defense Advanced Research Project Agency
- Dr. Douglas Maughan, Program Manager, U.S. Department of Homeland Security
- Gene Sokolowski, Assistant to the Director, Program Management and Technology, GSA
- Dr. Rick Summerhill, Associate Director, Internet2
- Marc Rotenberg, Executive Director, EPIC
- Ted Tanner, Jr., Architectural Strategist, Microsoft
- Rick White, President and Chief Executive Officer, TechNet

III. ADDITIONAL PARTICIPANTS

- CTIA
- Defense Advanced Research Project Agency (DARPA)
- U.S. Department of Defense
- U.S. Department of Homeland Security
- Federal Communications Commission
- IBM
- TechNet

REFERENCES

[1] The National Strategy to Secure Cyberspace, A/R 2-3, at 56 (Feb. 2003), at http://www.whitehouse.gov/pcipb/cyberspace_strategy.pdf.

[2] U.S. Dep't of Commerce, Census Bureau, "Quarterly Retail E-Commerce Sales 1st Quarter 2005, Table 4 (May 20, 2005), at http://www.census.gov/mrts/www/data/pdf/05Q1.pdf. Note that retail e-commerce sales may include some sales over proprietary networks, although such sales are presumably small at the retail level. Total e-commerce sales, including business-to-business sales, are much larger ($1.7 trillion in 2003—the last year for which Census Bureau data are available), but they include a larger percentage of sales over proprietary networks.

[3] See, e.g., Robert Litan and Alice Rivlin, "Projecting the Economic Impact of the Internet," 91 Am. Econ. Rev. 313 (2001) (noting studies suggesting the Internet can help government reduce the costs of receiving tax returns and registering for permits and licenses).

[4] A communications protocol defines the "[p]rocedures which are employed to ensure the orderly transfer of data between devices on a communications link, over a communications network, or within a system." NEWTON'S TELECOM DICTIONARY 196 (20th ed. 2004).

[5] IPv6 can be defined with reference to the IETF Requests for Comments (RFCs) that contain the relevant standards. The "core" draft standards for IPv6 (e.g., RFCs 2460-2463) were approved in August 1998. Currently, the suite of IETF documents that define IPv6 comprise more than 70 RFCs. See http://www.ietf.org/html.charters/ipv6-charter.html. The IETF continues its efforts to standardize the new protocol. See "WG Action: Recharter: IP Version 6 Working

Group (ipv6)," at http://www1.ietf.org/mail-archive/web/ietf-announce/current/msg00107.html (as modified May 5, 2004). For a brief discussion of the reasons for developing a next generation IP and the IETF's activities in that area, see Geoff Huston, "Waiting for IP version 6," at 1-4, The ISP Column (Jan. 2003), http://www.potaroo.net/ papers/isoc/2003-01/Waiting.html.

[6] Comments of Cisco Systems, Inc. (Cisco), at 1, in response to Request for Comments on Deployment of Internet Protocol Version 6, 69 Fed. Reg. 2,890 (U.S. Dep't of Commerce, National Institute of Standards and Technology [NIST] and National Telecommunications and Information Administration [NTIA] Jan. 21, 2004). Unless otherwise noted, all subsequent citations to Comments refer to comments filed in response to the January 21, 2004, Request for Comments (RFC). Copies of those comments are available at http://www.ntia.doc.gov/ntiahome/ntiageneral/ipv6/index.html. See also Tony Hain (Hain) Comments at 6.

[7] See, e.g., Cisco Comments at 1; MCI Comments at 3.

[8] See, e.g., Alcatel Comments at 3-4.

[9] See Cisco Comments at 6.

[10] See RFC, supra note Error! Bookmark not defined.6, 69 Fed. Reg. at 2,891-2,892, for a description of such address conservation mechanisms as network address translation (NAT) devices and Classless Intra-Domain Routing (CIDR). See also Sprint Corporation (Sprint) Comments at 4.

[11] An organization's incentive to convert to IPv6 on an expedited basis may be lessened further by the fact that IPv6 has been designed to allow IPv4 users to migrate to IPv6 on a gradual basis.

[12] See GSA Federal Technology Service (GSA) Comments at 3; Network Conceptions LLC (Network Conceptions) Comments at 9; VeriSign, Inc. (VeriSign) Comments at 6.

[13] Cisco Comments at 20; Juniper Networks, Inc. (Juniper) Comments at 5.

[14] See NTT/Verio Comments at 27. For purposes of this discussion, a network, a piece of equipment, or an application is considered "IPv6-capable" if it can recognize IPv6 addresses. Such devices, however, cannot process IPv6 messages until those IPv6 capabilities have been "enabled" or "turned on."

[15] Microsoft Corp. (Microsoft) Comments at 7-8. Windows XP was shipped with some IPv6 capabilities, and Microsoft representatives

have stated that the next release of Windows called "Vista," formally "Longhorn", will have IPv6 enabled by default.

[16] Cisco Comments at 20.

[17] Microsoft Comments at 8.

[18] See NTT/Verio Comments at 32-37 for a list of IPv6-capable hardware, operating systems, and software applications.

[19] See Cisco Comments at 20 (citing wired and wireless end user devices, cable and digital subscriber line (DSL) modems, printers and other peripheral equipment).

[20] As noted, IPv6-"capable" devices cannot process IPv6 messages until those IPv6 capabilities have been "enabled" or "turned on."

[21] See John Stenbit, "Internet Protocol Version 6 (IPv6)" (U.S. Dep't of Defense memorandum of intent, June 9, 2003), at http://ipv6.disa.mil/docs/stenbit-memo-20030609.pdf. All IPv6 equipment must also be able to support IPv4. See also Dawn S. Onley, "Defense picks consultant for IPv6 transition," Government Computer News, at 5 (May 24, 2004) at http://www.gcn.com/23-12/inbrief/26003-1.html. To date, however, DoD has not yet defined what IPv6-capable is. See William Jackson, "IPv.6-capable? That depends on your definition of "capable", Government Computer News (May 25, 2005), at http://www.gcn.com/vol1_no1/daily-updates/35912-1.html.

[22] See Stenbit, supra note 21, at 2 (indicating that no DoD networks carrying operational data will be converted to IPv6 in the near term); Captain Roswell V. Dixon, "IPv6 in the Department of Defense," at 9, Presentation at the North American IPv6 Task Force Summit, San Diego, CA, (June 25, 2003), http://www.usipv6.com/ppt/IPv6SummitPresentationFinalCaptDixon.pdf (DoD IPv6 adoption plan contemplates a five-year transition period with a trial period of approximately three years in which IPv6 and IPv4 will be operated simultaneously). A DoD official recently indicated that the department will not reach its original deadline for full transition to IPv6 by 2008. He further stated that DoD will likely continue to operate IPv4 alongside with IPv6 well into the next decade. See William Jackson, "DoD applications will have to wait for IPv6," Government Computer News (Nov. 30, 2005), at http://www.gcn.com/vol1_no1/daily-updates/37669-1.html (remarks of Kris Strance, a senior analyst with the Department's CIO office).

[23] See Internet2 Comments at 9 (Abilene network has supported native IPv6 since summer of 2002); Juniper Comments at 5.

[24] NTT/Verio Comments at 29. See also Cisco Comments at 20 (noting some private reports that other companies will provide IPv6 service if pressed).

[25] NTT/Verio Comments at 29.

[26] See "MCI takes step toward commercial IPv6 service," NetworkWorld Fusion (Feb. 7, 2005), at http://www.nwfusion.com/news/2005/020705-moonv6.html. NAv6TF is a subchapter of the IPv6 Forum dedicated to advancing and propagating IPv6 in North America. Acting as individuals, rather than as representatives of their employers, NAv6TF members provide technical leadership and innovative thought for the successful integration of IPv6 into all facets of networking and telecommunications infrastructure, present and future.

[27] See id.

[28] NTT/Verio Comments at 25; Juniper Comments at 6. In April 2001, NTT/Verio launched the first commercial global IPv6 backbone network connecting Japan, Europe, and the United States. NTT/Verio Comments at 25.

[29] NTT/Verio Comments at 25.

[30] Juniper Comments at 6.

[31] Prime Minister Yoshiro Mori, Policy Speech to the 150th Session of the Diet (Sept. 21, 2000),

[32] http://www.kantei.go.jp/foreign/souri/mori/2000/0921policy.html. For further information on Japan's IPv6 activities, see "e-Japan Strategy," at http://www.kantei.go.jp/foreign/it/network/0122full_e.html (Jan. 22, 2001). See also IPv6 Promotion Council, "Our Background and Objectives" (2002), at http://www.v6pc.jp/en/council/detail/index.html (last visited Dec. 15, 2004).

[33] See Sangjin Jeong, "IPv6 Deployment and its Testing Activities in Korea," at 9 (Sep. 22, 2003), at http://www.ipv6event.be/v6kim.pdf.

[34] See Cisco Comments at 22; Juniper Comments at 6. It has been reported that 50 percent of the CNGI project will go to local vendors. Cisco Comments at 22.

[35] See "Europe Drives Next Generation Internet Deployment," at http://www.euro6ix.org/press/Joint_Press_Release_v12.pdf (Dec. 4, 2001).

[36] See Juniper Comments at 6; Jordi Palet, "IPv6 in Europe: From RandD to Deployment" (June 2002), at http://usipv6.com/6sense/2004/jun/june.htm (last visited Jul. 15, 2005).

[37] See William Jackson, "Europe begins its move toward IPv6," Government Computer News (May 26, 2005), at http://www.gcn.com/vol1_no1/daily-updates/35915-1.html. For additional information on IPv6 activities in other nations, see U.S. General Accountability Office, Internet Protocol Version 6: Federal Agencies Need to Plan for Transition and Manage Security Risks, GAO-05-471, at 8-9 (May 2005), at http://www.gao.gov/new.items/d05471.pdf.
[38] See, e.g., NTT/Verio Comments at 25.
[39] See, e.g., Nobuo Ikeda and Hajime Yamada, "Is IPv6 Necessary?", Glocom Tech Bulletin #2, at 2, 12 (Feb. 27, 2002), at http://www.glocom.org/tech_reviews/tech_bulle/20020227_bulle_s2/index.html; Motorola, Inc. (Motorola) Comments at 5; Michael Dillon (Dillon) Comments at 1. See also Cisco Comments at 22 (Chinese carriers may feel political pressure to showcase China as a technology leader).
[40] See RFC, supra note Error! Bookmark not defined.6.
[41] "Technical and Economic Assessment of Internet Protocol Version 6 (IPv6)" (July 2004), at
[42] http://www.ntia.doc.gov/ntiahome/ntiageneral/ipv6/draft/discussiondraftv13_07162004.pdf.
[43] For information about the agenda of the meeting and a list of the participants, see NTIA's website, http://www.ntia.doc.gov/ntiahome/ntiageneral/ipv6/IPv6agenda_07272004.pdf. See also "IPv6 Public Meeting," 69 Fed. Reg. 42,422 (July 15, 2004). A transcript of the meeting (hereinafter referred to in this report as "Public Meeting Transcript") is also available at: http://www.ntia.doc.gov/ntiahome/ntiageneral/ipv6/webcast.html. All subsequent citations to that transcript will refer to the Microsoft Word version of that document.
[44] Statement of the Honorable Karen S. Evans, Administrator for Electronic Government and Information Technology, Office of Management and Budget, Before the House Comm. on Government Reform 2-3 (June 29, 2005) at http://www.whitehouse.gov/omb/legislative/testimony/evans/evans052905.html (OMB House Government Reform Testimony). See also Memorandum from Karen S. Evans, Off. of E-Government and Information Technology, Off. Mgmt. and Budget, to Chief Information Officers, OMB Memorandum M-05-22 (Aug. 22, 2005) at http://www.whitehouse.gov/omb/memoranda/fy2005/m05-22.pdf (OMB IPv6 Policy Memorandum).
[45] U.S. General Accountability Office, Internet Protocol Version 6: Federal Agencies Need to Plan for Transition and Manage Security

Risks, GAO-05-471, at 8-9 (May 2005), at http://www.gao.gov/new.items/d05471.pdf (GAO IPv6 Report).

[46] See, e.g., Microsoft Comments at 4-6; Motorola Comments at 2-4.

[47] The timing of the transition from IPv4 to IPv6 for any particular adopter, as well as the existing network infrastructure, could dramatically affect the costs incurred and the benefits realized.

[48] See Microsoft Comments at 3 (4.3 billion addresses); Sprint Comments at 3 (same). Because some of these addresses are needed for administrative purposes, all 4.3 billion cannot be assigned for use by individuals or organizations.

[49] See Sprint Comments at 3 (1x1030 addresses for every person); Joe St. Sauver, "What's IPv6 . . . and Why Is It Gaining Ground?", at http://cc.uoregon.edu/cnews/spring2001/whatsipv6.html (last visited Dec. 15, 2004) (3.7x1021 addresses per square inch). As with IPv4 addresses, not all of these IPv6 addresses can be assigned to users.

[50] See, e.g., NTT/Verio Comments at 10-11 (identifying future applications that could benefit from expanded IPv6 address space).

[51] See North American IPv6 Task Force (NAv6TF) Comments at 4.

[52] See Cisco Comments at 1; MCI Comments at 3; Motorola Comments at 4; NTT/Verio Comments at 5, 10. In contrast, one commenter questions whether each new mobile device will need its own IP address. See Network Conceptions Comments at 7.

[53] See Cisco Comments at 2; Dillon Comments at 1; GSA Comments at 2, 6; NTT/Verio Comments at 10. See also Public Meeting Transcript, supra note 41, at 65 (remarks of Paul Liao, Panasonic USA) (availability of IPv6-addressable electronic equipment in the home could make it easier and cheaper for companies to deliver software upgrades that could expand or modify the capabilities of that equipment); id. at 48-49 (remarks of Paul Liao and Stan Barber, NTT/Verio) (IPv6-addressed taxicabs in Tokyo can inform meteorologists when the cabs' windshield wipers are on, providing the weathermen with more detailed information about rainfall patterns in the city).

[54] RIRs are responsible for allocating IP address space to organizations (and in some cases individuals) in their respective regions. The American Registry of Internet Numbers (ARIN) is the RIR for the United States.

[55] See VeriSign Comments at 2. Some address reclamation has occurred. Stanford University, which was originally allocated nearly 17 million IP addresses, restructured its network in 2000 and gave back a Class A

address block equal to approximately 16 million IP addresses. See Carolyn Marsan, "Stanford Move Rekindles 'Net Address Debate,'" NetworkWorldFusion (Jan. 24, 2000), at http://www.nwfusion.com/news/2000/0124ipv4.html.

[56] Currently, the American Registry of Internet Numbers (ARIN) policies state that unused address space designated for return should be returned as agreed to the upstream provider that allocated the addresses and that 80 percent of the numbering space allocated must be utilized before additional addresses are requested. See ARIN's Number Resource Policy Manual at §§ 4.2.2.1.4, 4.2.2.2.3, 4.2.4.1, 4.2.4.2 (Oct. 15, 2004), at http://www.arin.net/policy/.

[57] Id. § 6.3.5.

[58] See, e.g., Network Conceptions Comments at 1; Sprint Comments at 1.

[59] See Alcatel Comments at 2 (e.g., deployment of NATs, implementation of CIDR, use of Dynamic Host Configuration Protocol (DHCP)).

[60] See, e.g., Cisco Comments at 1. But see Public Meeting Transcript, supra note 41, at 55-56 (remarks of Latif Ladid, NAv6TF) (excluding addresses controlled by the U.S. government and about 100 companies, "U.S. economy has only about 10 percent of the [IPv4] address space worldwide which is less than what Europe has and almost the same number as Asia").

[61] See John Lui, "Exec: No Shortage of Net Addresses," CNET News.Com (June 24, 2003), at http://news.com.com/Exec+No+shortage+of+Net+addresses/2100-1028_3-1020653.html (interview with Paul Wilson, director general of the Asia-Pacific Information Centre (APNIC)); Ikeda and Yamada, supra note 38. Indeed, there are widely different estimates as to when the existing supply of IPv4 addresses may finally run out. See, e.g., Lui, supra (estimate of Paul Wilson); Geoff Huston Comments passim; NTT/Verio Comments at 2-10.

[62] See supra notes 53 and 54, and accompanying text.

[63] The policies that govern management of IP resources at the various RIRs, including address allocation, are developed by stakeholders from the Internet community. The RIRs themselves do not develop those policies. For example, according to ARIN's "Internet Resource Policy Process," any individual may submit a proposal to alter these existing policies. See ARIN, "Internet Resource Policy Evaluation Process," (Jan. 22, 2004), at http://www.arin.net/policy/ipep.html.

[64] Andrew McLaughlin, "Bad Journalism, IPv6 and the BBC," Circle ID (Nov. 7, 2003), http://www.circleid.com/article/369_0_1_0_C/.

[65] Lui, supra note 59.

[66] Steps taken to improve the allocation of IP addresses on a going-forward basis will not correct imbalances in past allocations. The relevant authorities may need to enact measures to reclaim previously allocated but unused addresses or address blocks.

[67] The Internet Corporation for Assigned Names and Numbers (ICANN) allocates blocks of IP addresses to each RIR according to established needs. It performs this function as a result of a contract with the U.S. Department of Commerce. See Dep't of Commerce, NTIA, "IANA Functions Purchase Order," at http://www.ntia.doc.gov/ntiahome/domainname/iana.htm. When an RIR requires more IP addresses for allocation or assignment within its region, IANA makes an additional allocation to the RIR. End users in the U.S. are assigned addresses by ISPs, which obtain addresses from the RIR serving the United States, ARIN. See Internet Assigned Numbers Authority, "IP Address Services," at http://www.iana.org/ipaddress/ip-addresses.htm (last modified Apr. 12, 2005). Deployment of IPv6 addresses through this process began in 1999. In July 2004, ICANN added IPv6 to the root DNS zone, thereby enabling those servers to handle such addresses. Soon thereafter, the top-level domains of Japan and Korea (.jp and .kr, respectively) became the first to support IPv6. See ICANN, "Next-Generation IPv6 Addresses Added to the Internet's Root DNS Zone" (July 20, 2004), at

[68] http://www.icann.org/announcements/announcement-20jul04.htm; John Blau, "ICANN adds IPv6 to root servers," Computerworld (July 22, 2004),

[69] http://www.computerworld.com.au/index.php/id;586624082;fp;4;fpid;78268965.

[70] NAv6TF Comments at 34.

[71] VeriSign Comments at 2, 8.

[72] See NEWTON'S TELECOM DICTIONARY 563 (20th ed. 2004). Because NATs use port address translation (PAT), NAT/PAT could be used where NAT is referenced in this discussion.

[73] See Hain Comments at 3.

[74] See id. at 11.

[75] RTI Telephone Conversation with Rod Wallace, IPv6 Leader, Office of the Chief Technology Officer, and Elwyn Davies, IPv6 Technologist, Nortel Networks (Oct. 10, 2003) ("Nortel Discussion").

[76] Hain Comments at 2. See also Cisco Comments at 8 (unfettered E2E communications will allow for more rapid prototyping of new services, which is critical to developing those services); Alcatel Comments at 3; MCI Comments at 3.

[77] See, e.g., Public Meeting Transcript, supra note 41, at 60 (remarks of Tony Hain, Cisco) (removing NATs would allow companies to redirect personnel resources currently used to create work-arounds for particular applications towards development of the applications themselves); id. at 132 (remarks of Rick Summerhill, Internet2) (elimination of NATs would simplify the writing of applications software).

[78] See Cisco Comments at 5-6 (work-arounds scale well in most consumer markets, less well for enterprises and service providers).

[79] See Internet2 Comments at 4. The task of creating work-arounds typically must be repeated for each new application and frequently for different types of NATs.

[80] See, e.g., Cisco Comments at 9.

[81] See id. at 2; Internet2 Comments at 2-3; Microsoft Comments at 5; NAv6TF Comments at 6.

[82] See, e.g., Internet2 Comments at 1-2.

[83] See, e.g., OMB House Government Reform Testimony, supra note 42, at 1.

[84] RTI's estimates are based on Census Department data on automobile and appliance manufacturing and repair. Some of this remote monitoring capability is of course available today through unidirectional communications (i.e., from the appliance to the service provider) that do not require that the appliance be uniquely addressable. These applications would not need the expanded address space afforded by IPv6, or the removals of any NATs between the appliance and service provider.

[85] See, e.g., Marjory S. Blumenthal and David D. Clark, "Rethinking the design of the Internet: the end-to-end model vs. the brave new world," 1 ACM Transactions on Internet Technology 70, 71, 92-93 (2001), available at

[86] http://cybersecurity.stanford.edu/forum/files/blumenthal_clark.pdf.

[87] See BellSouth Comments at 4-5. See also Interview by RTI with John Streck, Centaur Labs, Research Triangle Park, N.C. (Mar. 16, 2004) ("March Streck Interview") (likelihood of the world, or even United States alone, moving completely back to the "open architecture" Internet model is not very high).

[88] Additionally, by reducing the number of "public" Internet addresses that an organization may need, use of NATs can reduce that organization's payments to Internet service providers (ISPs) for address space. See Public Meeting Transcript, supra note 41, at 15-16 (remarks of Vint Cerf, MCI) (indicating that his cable company allotted each customer one IP address and charged $5 per month for each additional address).

[89] See Alcatel Comments at 4; NTT/Verio Comments at 13-14.

[90] See Cisco Comments at 5.

[91] See infra Section 3.

[92] See Public Meeting Transcript, supra note 41, at 15 (remarks of Vint Cerf, MCI), 58 (remarks of Paul Francis, Cornell University), 178 (remarks of Preston Marshall, DARPA).

[93] NAT boxes and firewalls can be modified, albeit at some cost, to coexist in an IPv6 networked environment, possibly allowing some forms of direct E2E communications to take place. March Streck Interview, supra note 82.

[94] For an IETF working document that describes how mobility support can be provided in IPv6, see D. Johnson, et al., "Mobility Support in IPv6" (June 30, 2003), at

[95] http://users.piuha.net/jarkko/publications/mipv6/drafts/mobilev6.html (expired Dec. 29, 2003) (last visited May 2, 2005).

[96] NTT/Verio Comments at 10.

[97] Sprint Comments at 11.

[98] Thus, devices commonly found in the home (such as lights, dishwashers, refrigerators, cameras, home computers, and other home appliances) can be assigned IP addresses, linked together on home networks, and connected to the Internet, allowing home owners to control such devices remotely. See Motorola Comments at 4; March Streck Interview, supra note 82.

[99] Cisco suggests that IPv4 networks can also handle any mobile applications that exist today. Cisco believes, however, that a large scale deployment of mobile IP "will be done more easily through Mobile IPv6 and its feature set." Cisco Comments at 6.

[100] Microsoft Comments at 5.

[101] NAv6TF Comments at 12-13. The autoconfiguration and neighbor discovery mechanisms of IPv6, which are used for node discovery, also eliminate the need for DHCP or foreign agents currently used to route mobile traffic. See Wolfgang Fritsche and Florian Heissenhuber,

"Mobile IPv6: Mobility Support for the Next Generation Internet," at 18 (Aug. 16, 2000), at

[102] http://www.6bone.sk/zaujim/MobileIPv6_Whitepaper.pdf.

[103] Sprint Comments at 6. The mobility protocols within IPv6 are designed to avoid routing packets from a correspondent node to the mobile node via the home agent. This route optimization mechanism will reduce transport delay and save network capacity. Route optimization is designed to be an integral part of Mobile IPv6 and is also available as an added functionality for Mobile IPv4. See Fritsche and Heissenhuber, supra note 95, at 18.

[104] For example, a laptop linked to the Internet at home could be carried to work and then connected to the Internet there. Alternatively, a mobile phone user, who is browsing the Web, could remain seamlessly connected to the Internet while traveling from Boston to New York by linking to networks along the way. In both cases users can be reached by simply querying their home IP addresses.

[105] An improved ability to provide such seamless mobility services will likely be a significant incentive for mobile service providers to deploy IPv6. See, e.g., Public Meeting Transcript, supra note 41, at 69-70 (remarks of Mark Desautels, CTIA).

[106] See Wikipedia: The Free Encyclopedia, "Internet Protocol", at http://en.wikipedia.org/wiki/Internet_Protocol (last modified Nov. 29, 2004).

[107] See hyperdictionary, "Quality of Service: Dictionary Entry and Meaning," at

[108] http://www.hyperdictionary.com/search.aspx?define=quality+of+servi ce (last visited Dec. 21, 2004) (quality of service is "the performance properties of a network service, possibly including throughput, transit delay, and priority").

[109] See Hain Comments at 3; Internet2 Comments at 3-4.

[110] See Protocol Dictionary, "IPv6 (IPng): Internet Protocol version 6," at http://www.javvin.com/protocolIPv6.html (last visited Dec. 21, 2004).

[111] S. Deering and R. Hinden, "Internet Protocol, Version 6 (IPv6) Specification," 30 (Dec. 1998), at http://www.ietf.org/rfc/rfc2460.txt.

[112] Lawrence Roberts, "QoS Signaling for IPv6," § 1.1, at 2 (Dec. 11, 2003), http://ftp.tiaonline.org/tr-34/tr3417/Working/Dec-03 (last visited July 16, 2004) (document is only available with a password).

[113] J. Rajahalme, et al., "IPv6 Flow Level Specification," Internet Society, RFC 3697 (March 2004), at ftp://ftp.rfc-editor.org/in-notes/ rfc3697.txt. A "flow" is "a sequence of packets sent from a particular

source to a particular . . . destination that the source desires to label as a flow." Id. at 1 (§ 1).

[114] See id. at 2 (§1).

[115] See id. at 3 (§ 4) ("To enable flow-specific treatment, flow state needs to be established on all or a subset of the IPv6 nodes on the path from the source to the destination(s)."). The presence of NATs may also complicate deployment of QoS. See Internet2 Comments at 4.

[116] March Streck Interview, supra note 82. The cost to upgrade to IPv6 and adjust a network to use the capabilities of IPv6 (e.g., remove NATs) could be very costly depending on the specific setup of a particular network.

[117] See Cisco Comments at 5; GSA Comments at 6; Microsoft Comments at 5; Sprint Comments at 8. See also Public Hearing Transcript, supra note 41, at 57 (remarks of Latif Ladid, NAv6TF) (research by Forrester Research Group suggests that autoconfiguration could pay for IPv6 implementation within one year). With autoconfiguration, a user can simply plug a host device into the network and it will automatically configure an IP address and network prefix and find all available routers. GSA Comments at 6.

[118] See Cisco Comments at 4.

[119] See Internet2 Comments at 2-3 ("expert ISP engineers and ordinary users have their time wasted trying to debug network problems either caused by the NAT boxes or made more difficult to diagnose by the NAT boxes").

[120] NAv6TF notes that voice and data are converging into one platform. NAv6TF Comments at 23. If middleware, such as gateways and NATs, is required everywhere, the cost for single-vendor solutions may be containable, but multi-vendor solutions will be costly interoperability propositions.

[121] See Cisco Comments at 4.

[122] See infra Section 2.2 for more information on the sorts of costs that may be incurred in the transition to IPv6.

[123] This conclusion is based on RTI's analysis of RFC comments, extensive literature reviews, and discussions with stakeholders and experts.

[124] See March Streck Interview, supra note 82.

[125] Network processing to maintain NAT translation tables can cause a bottleneck if network traffic grows very rapidly.

[126] In this statement, "routing tables" generally refers to backbone routers and national DNS routing tables. As the number of IP addresses has

grown, these routing tables have tracked individual IP addresses rather than utilizing hierarchical mapping, in which one IP address can afford entry to many others. In IPv6 routing tables, a more hierarchical approach could be used to reduce the size of backbone routing tables, as well as those of all routers. The potential network efficiency gains, however, would be experienced at the backbone level.

[127] March Streck Interview, supra note 82.

[128] For a case study of how and at what pace an enterprise might adopt IPv6 and the sorts of costs it would likely incur, see Appendix A.

[129] This assumes that adoption occurs after routine cyclical upgrades provide IPv6 capabilities in hardware and software to the user community.

[130] This conclusion is based on RTI's analysis of RFC comments, extensive literature reviews, and discussions with stakeholders and experts See also Cisco Comments at 10 (as IPv6 becomes more prevalent, "customers will be able to transition based on their need to do so without excessive regard to hardware costs").

[131] See also Hain Comments at 11; NAv6TF Comments at 28; Public Hearing Transcript, supra note 41, at 62 (remarks of Stan Barber, NTT/Verio) (labor costs will be the most significant deployment cost, but the costs will be mitigated if the labor force is familiar with IPv4).

[132] Nortel Discussion, supra note 71.

[133] See Cisco Comments at 27; Motorola Comments at 5-6. See Section 4 infra for more information on interoperability costs and considerations.

[134] See Cisco Comments at 21; Hain Comments at 8-10; NAv6TF Comments at 21, 36, 43; NTT/Verio Comments at 28.

[135] See BellSouth Comments at 6; Cisco Comments at 13.

[136] See Cisco Comments at 13. See infra Section 2.4 for more detail on such "first-mover" considerations.

[137] See Cisco Comments at 13; Dillon Comments at 1.

[138] See supra notes 19-27 and accompanying text.

[139] See NAv6TF Comments at 24.

[140] "Tunneling" is a technology that enables one network to send its data via another network's connections. Tunneling works by encapsulating a network protocol within packets carried by the second network. Isp.webopedia.com, "Tunneling" at http://isp.webopedia.com/TERM/T/tunneling.html (last visited Dec. 21, 2004). In the IPv6 context, an ISP would "tunnel" by encapsulating an IPv6 message in an IPv4 packet, enabling that message to be routed to an IPv6-enabled host via

an IPv4 network. Firms could establish such IPv6-to-IPv4 on their own, or ask a so-called "tunnel broker" to establish the necessary connection.

[141] RTI Telephone conversation with Joe Houle, Technology Consultant, IP Network Architecture, ATandT, in Arlington, VA (Dec. 11, 2003).

[142] Id.

[143] Id.

[144] March Streck Interview, supra note 82.

[145] See Cisco Comments at 13.

[146] NTT/Verio is not providing IPv4 to IPv6 or IPv6 to IPv4 service; therefore, customers would need to maintain dual-stack networks themselves or integrate translation techniques to continue to communicate with IPv4 networks.

[147] NTT/Verio Comments at 21.

[148] See, e.g., Cisco Comments at 12.

[149] See id.

[150] Some experts have stated that certain inadequacies exist in IPv6 standards, such as management information base and billing systems specifications, and that others may develop as IPv6 testing continues. See id. at 17; NAv6TF Comments at 32-33.

[151] RTI Telephone Conversation with Rick Summerhill, Director, Network Research, Architecture and Technology, Internet2 (Nov. 5, 2003) ("Internet2 Discussion). Internet2 is a network of approximately 200 educational and institutional Internet users. The 11 backbone routers that support the Internet2 network have recently been upgraded to new Juniper routers, which are dual-stack with IPv4- and IPv6-enabled hardware.

[152] See Hain Comments at 11.

[153] See BellSouth Comments at 5.

[154] See, e.g., Cisco Comments at 10, 12.

[155] See BellSouth Comments at 6; Dillon Comments at 2; Hain Comments at 11. Cisco additionally indicated that these costs can be amortized over a gradual development cycle. Cisco Comments at 11.

[156] See GSA Comments at 8; Hain Comments at 13, 14-15; NAv6TF Comments at 28. See also Public Hearing Transcript, supra note 41, at 62 (remarks of Stan Barber, NTT/Verio) (labor costs will be the most significant deployment cost, but the costs will be mitigated if the labor force is familiar with IPv4).

[157] See Cisco Comments at 12.

[158] See NAv6TF Comments at 29.

[159] Once dual-stack capabilities are enabled by default in a host operating system (e.g., as Microsoft plans to do in the next version of Windows, see Microsoft Comments at 8), the user should not be aware whether IPv4 or IPv6 packets are being sent or received. Thus, no training should be necessary, unless new IPv6-specific applications are requested by users.

[160] See BellSouth Comments at 6; Cisco Comments at 12; Hain Comments at 16.

[161] See BellSouth Comments at 6; Cisco Comments at 13.

[162] See, e.g., Ikeda and Yamada, supra note 38, at 2, 12; Hain Comments at 1; Motorola Comments, at 5; Dillon Comments at 1. See also Cisco Comments at 22 (Chinese carriers may feel political pressure to showcase China as a technology leader).

[163] See Alcatel Comments at 2; Cisco Comments at 24; Hain Comments at 8; NAv6TF Comments at 6-7.

[164] First-mover advantages arise from four general factors: (1) technology leadership, (2) preemption of scarce resources or assets, (3) scale economies producing an ability to charge lower prices, thereby expanding market share, and (4) an ability to "lock in" users due to the high costs of switching to alternative technologies or products. See Marvin B. Lieberman and David B. Montgomery, "First-Mover Advantages," 9 Strategic Mgmt. J. 41 (1988).

[165] See Paul Stoneman, The Economics of Technological Diffusion 50-51 (Blackwell Publishing 2001). Monopoly profits which are frequently captured by innovators for a period of time are the reward for risk taking and provide the risk capital for investment in the next generation of the technology.

[166] See David Needle, "The Myth of the First Mover Advantage," siliconvalley.internet.com (Apr. 5, 2000), at http://siliconvalley.internet.com/news/article.php/3541_333311.

[167] The term "spillover" refers to the fact that some benefits of a particular economic activity (e.g., RandD) frequently accrue ("spill over") to parties other than the one that originally undertook the activity. "Information" or "knowledge spillovers" result from the movement of information from the originating firm to other producers (e.g., through publication of the originating firm's basic research, through "reverse engineering" of the originating firm's product by other firms, or by the movement of employees from the originating firm to other organizations). "Market spillovers" result when the operation of the market for a new product or process causes some of the benefits

thereby created to flow to producers and consumers other than the innovating firm. See, e.g., Bronwyn H. Hall, "The Private and Social Returns to Research and Development", in Technology, RandD, and the Economy 140-141 (Bruce L.R. Smith and Claude E. Barfield, eds., 1995); Adam B Jaffe, "The Importance of 'Spillovers' in the Policy Mission of the Advanced Technology Program," 23 J. Tech. Transfer 11, 11-12 (1998), available at http://www.atp.nist.gov/eao/jtt/jaffe.pdf; Zvi Griliches, "The Search for RandD Spillovers," NBER Working Paper No. 3768 (Nat'l Bur. Economic Res. 1991), available at http://nber.org/papers/w3768.pdf.

[168] See Gerard J. Tellis and Peter N. Golder, "First to Market, First to Fail: Real Causes of Enduring Market Leadership," 37 MIT Sloan Mgmt. Rev. 65 (1996).

[169] "Infratechnologies" are a diverse set of technical tools that are necessary to conduct efficiently all phases of RandD, to control production processes, and to execute marketplace transactions for complex technology-based goods. Examples include measurement and test methods, process and quality control techniques, evaluated scientific and engineering data, and the technical basis for product interfaces. These tools are called infratechnologies because they provide a complex but essential technical infrastructure. Many infratechnologies are adopted as industry standards, emphasizing their public good content. See Gregory Tassey, "Standardization in Technology-Based Markets," 29 Res. Pol. 587, 595-597 (2000).

[170] See, e.g., Motorola Comments at 8-9; Public Hearing Transcript, supra note 41, at 172 (remarks of Rick White, TechNet).

[171] See Tassey, supra note 161, at 590-593.

[172] See Alcatel Comments at 4; Hain Comments at 17-18; Lockheed Comments at 5; NAv6TF Comments at 6-7. But see Public Meeting Transcript, supra note 41, at 167-168 (remarks of Rick White, TechNet) (questioning whether "lag" in U.S. deployment of IPv6 as compared to other countries would raise competitiveness concerns).

[173] Internet2 Discussion, supra note 143 (designing the next generation of Internet applications will be simpler in IPv6 because developers will not need to build on the more than 20 years of work-arounds embedded in IPv4).

[174] See Alcatel Comments at 4 (RandD activities could be diluted because new products and services will need to be dual protocol compatible, potentially causing U.S. companies to lag behind in developing next generation IPv6 applications). On the other hand, given that IPv4 and

IPv6 will likely coexist for a lengthy period of time, equipment manufacturers and applications designers may be constrained to develop both IPv4 and IPv6-compatible products. Cf. Public Meeting Transcript, supra note 41, at 68-69 (remarks of Stan Barber, NTT/Verio) (emphasizing the importance of devising security tools that work with both IPv4 and IPv6).

[175] See, e.g., Hain Comments at 10-12.

[176] See Motorola Comments at 2; NAv6TF Comments at 46.

[177] See, e.g., Microsoft Comments at 12 n.8.

[178] RTI Telephone Conversation with John Streck, Centaur Labs (May 18, 2004).

[179] NTT/Verio Comments at 13. See also Microsoft Comments at 11 (IPv6 is a "new, more secure protocol" that could help make North America a "Safe Cyber Zone").

[180] See, e.g., Cisco Comments at 3; GSA Comments at 6; MCI Comments at 4. IPsec is a set of protocols developed by the IETF to support the secure exchange of packets at the IP layer. IPsec has been deployed widely to implement Virtual Private Networks (VPNs). IPsec consists of two optional security headers: Encapsulating Security Payload (ESP), which can provide both encryption and integrity-protection, and Authentication Header (AH), which provides only integrity-protection. The ESP header is more widely used. Both headers support two modes—transport and tunnel. In transport mode using ESP, IPsec protects only the data portion (payload) of each packet but leaves the header untouched. In tunnel mode with ESP, IPsec protects both the payload and the inner header (that of the ultimate recipient), but leaves the outer header untouched. On the receiving side, an IPsec-compliant device decrypts and authenticates each packet. For IPsec to work, the sending and receiving devices must agree on secret (symmetric) keys, which are used to provide encryption and integrity-protection. This is accomplished through a protocol known as Internet Key Exchange (IKE), which also allows the peers to mutually authenticate using digital certificates or other methods, and which negotiates the IPsec protections to be provided and the cryptographic algorithms to be used. See internet.com Webopedia, "IPsec," at http://www.webopedia.com/TERM/I/IPsec.html (last visited July 12, 2005).

[181] BellSouth Comments at 3.

[182] See Cisco Comments at 3; Public Hearing Transcript, supra note 41, at 77-78 (remarks of Latif Ladid, NAv6TF). In order to fully realize this benefit of the IPv6 address space, care must be taken to avoid overly

simplistic interface ID assignments (e.g., sequential, embedded IPv4 addresses). The benefit can be best realized in large networks by employing random privacy addresses or cryptographically generating addresses.

[183] Lawrence A. Gordov, et al., "2004 CSI/FBI Computer Crime and Security Survey" at 10, at http://www.reddshell.com/docs/csi_fbi_2004.pdf (last visited July 12, 2005). Additionally, at least 45 percent of respondents reported spending three percent or more of their IT budget on security, and approximately 53 percent of respondents reported unauthorized use of computer systems within the last 12 months. Id. at 4 (Fig. 5), 8 (Fig. 11).

[184] See, e.g., Alcatel Comments at 4; BellSouth Comments at 3; Cisco Comments at 3, 17; Internet2 Comments at 3; VeriSign Comments at 9. Although most parties believe that increased use of IPsec will improve security, other commenters are less certain. Motorola asserts that IPsec, in its current form, cannot defend against denial of service attacks. Motorola Comments at 4. BellSouth questions whether IPsec can strictly eliminate "spoofing." BellSouth Comments at 4. More broadly, VeriSign suggests that IPsec may have been rendered irrelevant by the rise of attacks and security threats for which IPsec-based solutions are either unhelpful or counterproductive. VeriSign Comments at 2. Other commenters note that IPsec provides only network-level security and, as a result, may need to be supplemented by other measures. See Alcatel Comments at 3 (need to secure critical subsystems such as neighbor discovery and routing); Electronic Privacy Information Center (EPIC) Comments at 2 (need to secure applications).

[185] See Qwest Communications International Inc. (Qwest) Comments at 4; VeriSign Comments at 2.

[186] See BellSouth Comments at 3; Cisco Comments at 3; Internet2 Comments at 3.

[187] See Internet2 Comments at 3; MCI Comments at 5. Cisco asserts that work-arounds are becoming available that will permit E2E IPsec even across NATs. Cisco Comments at 3.

[188] Some commenters suggest that the removal of NATs to implement IPsec fully may reduce security for some users. See, e.g., Motorola Comments at 3. Other commenters suggest that deployment of IPv6 may be hindered by the absence of IPv6-compatible security "tools" (e.g., firewalls, intrusion detection systems). See Public Meeting Transcript, supra note 41, at 80 (remarks of Stan Barber, NTT/Verio),

147-148 (remarks of Marilyn Kraus, Department of Defense). Development and deployment of such tools, like the continued use of NATs, may interfere with E2E communications using IPsec.

[189] See Cisco Comments at 14; Network Conceptions Comments at 9.

[190] The maximum transmission unit (MTU) is a link layer restriction on the maximum number of bytes of data in a single transmission (i.e., frame, cell, packet, depending on the terminology). See Marc Slemko, "Path MTU Discovery and Filtering ICMP," at http://alive.znep.com/~marcs/mtu/ (last modified Nov. 12, 1998).

[191] The IETF has taken steps to address some of these concerns through the development of specifications for secure neighbor discovery and cryptographically generated addresses (CGAs). Additional work remains to complete additional specifications (e.g., proxy neighbor discovery) and define best common practices for the secure use of IPv6 auto-configuration capabilities. While IPv4 makes less extensive and required use of auto-configuration technologies, its control protocols (e.g., ARP, ICMP) have many similar vulnerabilities to insider attacks and abuse, but there is little development on the horizon to address the issues in a manner similar to IPv6. See generally Sean Covery and Darrin Miller, "IPv6 and IPv4 Threat Comparison and Best-Practice Evaluation (v1.0)" at 9, 15-16 (appended to Cisco Comments).

[192] See Internet Security Alliance (ISA) Comments at 2.

[193] See, e.g., Public Hearing Transcript, supra note 41, at 59 (remarks of Latif Ladid, NAV6TF), 149-151 (remarks of Preston Marshall, DARPA).

[194] Perimeter-based networks can also extend security protections further into the network (i.e., "defense in depth"). More commonly, there are few explicit security mechanisms at the lowest levels of the protected network (e.g., individual hosts or work stations), instead relying on "local trust" at the subnet, or site level. One obvious ramification of this approach is that at some level, insider threats may well go undetected and undeterred.

[195] See Public Hearing Transcript, supra note 41, at 156-157 (remarks of Preston Marshall, DARPA). The deployment of IPv6 itself may contribute to the obsolescence of traditional perimeter security architectures because many of its capabilities (e.g., end-to-end connectivity, tunneling, encryption), if enabled, make perimeter control of network communications difficult. Basic IPv6 packet

construction also complicates inspection of its data by security middleboxes.

[196] See Richard Graveman, "IPv6 Security Top Ten – A Quick Warm-Up Exercise," at 5 (Nov. 2004), available at http://www.ipv6seminar.com/index.html (on file with author).

[197] See, e.g., Verisign, Inc., "Understanding PKI," at http://verisign.netscape.com/security/pki/understanding.html (last visited Dec. 21, 2004).

[198] See BellSouth Comments at 3; Cisco Comments at 3; Hain Comments at 4; NAv6TF Comments at 9; NTT/Verio Comments at 15.

[199] See BellSouth Comments at 4.

[200] See id. at 3-4.

[201] See NTT/Verio Comments at 16. This tension mirrors that experienced by users and network administrators. Although implementation of IPsec allows users to protect the secrecy of their communications traffic, IPsec encryption can reduce security for network administrators by denying them the ability to monitor the content of each packet stream for hostile content. See Hain Comments at 4. IPsec-based packet encryption may also defeat network security screening activities by firewalls and intruder detection systems.

[202] See Cisco Comments at 3. Enhanced traceability could make it more difficult to engage in anonymous online conduct. See EPIC Comments at 2-3.

[203] See NTT/Verio Comments at 13-14.

[204] See EPIC Comments at 3.

[205] See Cisco Comments at 4.

[206] See NTT/Verio Comments at 16.

[207] See S. Roy, A. Durand, and J. Paugh, "Issues with Dual Stack IPv6 on by Default," at 10 (§ 3.3) (July 7, 2004), at http://www.ietf.org/proceedings/04aug/I-D/draft-ietf-v6ops-v6onbydefault-03.txt.

[208] See id. See also United States Computer Emergency Readiness Team, "US-CERT Federal Informational Notice FIN05-095," at 1 (Apr. 5, 2005), at http://www.us-cert.gov/federal/archive/infoNotices/FIN05-095.html (on file with author). Attackers can also use IPv6-to-IPv4 translation to hide their identity and location and thus defeat defensive traceback efforts. Covery and Miller, supra note 183, at 20 (§ 3.1.9.1).

[209] Covery and Miller, supra note 183, at 19 (§ 3.1.9.1).

[210] See Michael Warfield, "Security Implications of IPv6," at 29 (Nov. 2004), available at http://www.ipv6seminar.com/index.html (on file with author).

[211] March Streck Interview, supra note 82. See also "Domain addresses limitless, expert says," Toronto Star, July 21, 2004, at E4 (Vint Cerf suggests that IPv6 will run parallel with IPv4 for about 20 years).
[212] See, e.g., Hain Comments at 10, 12.
[213] See id. at 10.
[214] See Cisco Comments at 17.
[215] See Hain Comments at 19; Lockheed Comments at 4-5; Motorola Comments at 9-10. Some commenters expressed the concern that flexibility in how IPsec is implemented could limit its effectiveness. See Hain Comments at 3-4; NAv6TF Comments at 35-36.
[216] See NAv6TF Comments at 24.
[217] See Roy, Durand, and Paugh, supra note 199, at 1.
[218] See Hain Comments at 10 (tunneling increases overhead by 10 percent).
[219] See Cisco Comments at 12-13.
[220] See Public Meeting Transcript, supra note 41, at 136 (remarks of Rick White, TechNet).
[221] See Alcatel Comments at 2.
[222] See BellSouth Comments at 6.
[223] See, e.g., Alcatel Comments at 2, 4-5.
[224] See Cisco Comments at 16.
[225] Network externalities arise from the fact that the value of a network to its users typically increases with the number of people that can access the network. Similarly, networking effects arise from the fact that the value of a network also increases with the number of individuals actually using the network. When a consumer decides whether to purchase and use a networked product or service (such as an IPv6-capable device), that person considers only the personal benefits of that purchase, and ignores the benefits conferred on all other users (e.g., those users who may now have a new opponent in a IPv6-based gaming service). The individual may choose not to purchase the networked product or service, even though that purchase may have increased overall economic welfare. In consequence, deployment of the service (and the equipment and technologies that make that service possible) will be less than it "should" be. See Michael Parkin, Economics 504-510 (Addison-Wesley 1990); Robert Willig, "The Theory of Network Access Pricing," in Issues in Public Utility Regulation 109 and n.2 (H. M. Trebbing ed., 1979).
[226] The theoretical and empirical literature concludes that the presence of market failures will tend to cause private-sector firms to underinvest in

RandD. For a survey of that literature, see Stephen Martin and John T. Scott., "The Nature of Innovation Market Failure and the Design of Public Support for Private Innovation," 29 Res. Pol. 437 (Apr. 2000), available at http://www.mgmt.purdue.edu/faculty/smartin/vita/9902.pdf. See Gregory Tassey, "Underinvestment in Public Good Technologies," 30 J. Tech. Transfer 90-94 (2005).

[227] See Tassey, supra note 218, at 105-108.

[228] See Internet2 Comments at 9; Motorola Comments at 9.

[229] See Lockheed Comments at 3; Microsoft Comments at 12-13; Motorola Comments at 8; Qwest Comments at 1.

[230] See Cisco Comments at 25-26.

[231] See NAv6TF Comments at 37-38; Sprint Comments at 14.

[232] See Hain Comments at 20.

[233] See Public Meeting Transcript, supra note 41, at 141-142 (remarks of Rick White, TechNet)

[234] See Hain Comments at 18; Internet2 Comments at 2; Lockheed Comments at 6; Motorola Comments at 2-3.

[235] Once large-scale transition begins, most software would be IPv6 enabled within 24 months through general market forces. See Internet2 Comments at 2.

[236] See Cisco Comments at 25; Microsoft Comments at 9; NAv6TF Comments at 38; Qwest Comments at 2-3.

[237] See Lockheed Comments at 3; NAv6TF Comments at 38.

[238] See Tassey, supra note 161.

[239] This conclusion is based on RTI's analysis of the RFC comments, the relevant literature, and discussions with industry stakeholders.

[240] Government agencies have a proven history of working with private-sector organizations to provide conformance testing and validation certificates. For example, NIST recently led the selection and testing of the Advanced Encryption Standard (AES) that specifies a cryptographic algorithm for use by U.S. government organizations to protect sensitive (unclassified) information. It is anticipated that the AES will be used widely on a voluntary basis by organizations, institutions, and individuals outside of the U.S. government and outside of the United States. As part of the development process, algorithm testing was conducted under the Cryptographic Module Validation Program (CMVP), run jointly by NIST and the Communications Security Establishment (CSE) of the Government of Canada. Commercial, accredited laboratories also test cryptographic implementations for conformance to NIST's standards, and if the

implementations conform, then NIST and CSE issue jointly signed validation certificates for those implementations. See National Institute of Standards and Technology, Report on the Development of the Advanced Encryption Standard (AES) (Oct. 2002), at http://csrc.nist.gov/CryptoToolkit/aes/round2/r2report.pdf.

[241] See Motorola Comments at 2.

[242] See NAv6TF Comments at 24.

[243] MCI Comments at 6.

[244] In the 1990s, the government decided to initiate the GOSIP, or Government Open Systems Interconnection Profile, which was a mandate to force conformance with an Open Systems Interconnect (OSI) standard. In this instance, the U.S. Government mandated that all government agencies use GOSIP. According to RFC 1169, published by the Internet Architecture Board (IAB), GOSIP was "needed because OSI standards allow many potential options and choices, some of which are incompatible." V. Cerf and K. Mills, "RFC 1169—Explaining the Role of GOSIP" (Aug. 1990), at http://www.faqs.org/rfcs/rfc1169.html. Although more than 20 different agencies participated in developing the GOSIP specifications, few OSI applications ever became available; thus, government agencies generally continued to use and expand their use of the Internet Protocol Suite (IPS). In 1995, the Secretary of Commerce removed the mandate on OSI usage by government agencies. According to a bulletin released by NIST in May 1995, the Federal Internetworking Requirement Panel concluded that "federal government agencies should have flexibility to select networking protocol standards based on such factors as interoperability needs, existing infrastructure, costs, the availability of marketplace products, and status of a protocol suite as a standard." National Institute of Standards and Technology, "Standards For Open Systems: More Flexibility For Federal Users" (1995), at http://www.itl.nist.gov/lab

[245] bulletns/archives/b595.txt.

[246] RTI Telephone Conversation with John Streck, Centaur Labs (Sep. 14, 2004).

[247] See, e.g., BellSouth Comments at 9; Cisco Comments at 29; Microsoft Comments at 12-13.

[248] See Cisco Comments at 26-27; Microsoft Comments at 11.

[249] See, e.g., BellSouth Comments at 9.

[250] Public Meeting Transcript, supra note 41, at 135-137 (remarks of Rick White, TechNet).

[251] See Network Conceptions Comments at 23.

[252] See NAv6TF Comments at 43; Lockheed Comments at 2-3; Microsoft Comments at 12.

[253] See BellSouth Comments at 9; Cisco Comments at 28; Motorola Comments at 9; NAv6TF Comments at 44.

[254] See MCI Comments at 9.

[255] See, e.g., Lockheed Comments at 2; MCI Comments at 8; NAv6TF Comments at 42-43. See also OMB IPv6 Policy Memorandum, supra note 42.

[256] See, e.g., BellSouth Comments at 8; Dillon Comments at 3; Qwest Comments at 5-6.

[257] See, e.g., Lockheed Comments at 4.

[258] See Dillon Comments at 2.

[259] See Hain Comments at 13.

[260] See Cisco Comments at 29; Dillon Comments at 2; NAv6TF Comments at 45-46.

[261] See Cisco Comments at 28.

[262] See Hain Comments at 18.

[263] NAv6TF Comments at 45-46.

[264] See Cisco Comments at 28-29; Dillon Comments at 2; GSA Comments at 11; Internet2 Comments at 10; NAv6TF Comments at 45-46.

[265] GAO IPv6 Report, supra note 43, at 31.

[266] OMB Government Reform Testimony, supra note 42, at 2-3.

[267] Operating a dual IPv4/IPv6-capable network will be somewhat more costly than operating an IPv6 (or IPv4) only network. See Cisco Comments at 14-15; Hain Comments at 16-17.

[268] These users do not have network management software or major networking hardware which would need to be enabled. Routing upgrades would provide equipment and software that would be IPv6 enabled several years into the future, but no additional cost should be seen.

[269] This hypothetical builds on the discussion of IPv6 transition costs presented in Section 2.2 of the main report. It is also based on RTI's review of the RFC comments and its discussions with industry stakeholders and RTI's own networking staff.

[270] Tunneling refers to using tunneling techniques in one or more routers to enable IPv6 messages to traverse IPv4 networks, and running dual-stack operating systems on host computers. In order for any IPv6 applications to be used on IPv4-based computers, the operating system

on each computer will need to support both the IPv6 and IPv4 protocol stacks.

[271] As routine upgrades take place, IPv6 capabilities will be part of installed hardware and software both at the host level and at the network level, though not on the same timeframe. Although the capabilities have to be enabled, or "turned on," the level and timing of IPv6 capabilities will significantly affect transition costs.

[272] Microsoft's Teredo is a software application that allows an IPv6-over-IPv4 tunnel to originate at a Windows host, rather than at a router. Teredo encapsulate IPv6 packets within certain IPv4 packets, allowing messages from an IPv6 host device to be routed over IPv4 networks and even through IPv4 NATs. See Microsoft TechNet, "Teredo Overview," at

[273] http://www.microsoft.com/technet/prodtechnol/winxppro/maintain/teredo.mspx (last updated Jul. 30, 2004).

[274] During this phase, the majority of network management software and user software and applications will be IPv6-enabled.

INDEX

D

E

F

G

H

I

J

K

L

M

N

O

P

Q

R

S

T

U